THE TEDDY BEAR

LOVERS' BOOK

The most famous Teddy Bear lover of recent times and his bear: Anthony Andrews as Lord Sebastian Flyte with Aloysius in Brideshead Revisited.

THE TEDDY BEAR

LOVERS' BOOK

Philippa and Peter Waring

PICTORIAL PRESENTATIONS
SOUVENIR PRESS

By the same authors
IN PRAISE OF TEDDY BEARS

First published 1985 by Souvenir Press Ltd,
43 Great Russell Street, London WC1B 3PA
and simultaneously in Canada

ISBN 0 285 62729 5

Photoset and printed in Great Britain by
Photobooks (Bristol) Ltd.

Someone soft and warm
Someone quiet and understanding,
Always willing to listen
Always willing to play,
Anytime of the day
Always there,
Teddy Bear.

JUDITH ROBINS

For Ernest, Tessa and, of course, Colonel Bob

CONTENTS

The authors' hug of bears.

INTRODUCTION

This is 'The Year of the Teddy Bear', for not only has UNICEF chosen a teddy to symbolise its 'International Youth Year', but society in general and the manufacturing industry in particular has designated 1985 as the year of the bear.

Commenting on January 2, *The Times* declared, 'This, we are promised, will be the "Year of the Bear". Marketing men have set their sights on next Christmas for the Teddy Bear to supplant Cabbage Patch Dolls, and UNICEF is combining the year of youth and the year of the bear in common cause for the coming 365 days.'

And if you have any doubt about such a claim, take a look at the number of bears that have sprung up in shop windows, on lounge furniture and office desks, not to mention in cars, buses, caravans and on weekend boats. They are everywhere in advertising, turning up on radio and television, and hardly a day passes when they are not photographed and written about for some exploit in newspapers and magazines. Veteran bears have also become much sought after by collectors, and where once they were sold for pennies at jumble sales, they can now go for thousands of pounds at London and New York auctions. And, of course, this is not taking into account the millions upon millions of teddies resting comfortably in bedrooms or quietly snoozing away their retirement after the rigors of their owners' childhood!

It has all come about because the world is now 'bear aware'. People everywhere have become conscious that the Teddy Bear is more than just a toy, more than just a childhood plaything to be discarded in adulthood. Teddy can be a life-long friend, too, with a very significant role to play in his or her owner's life.

Two happy arctophiles at the launching party for the authors' previous book in 1980.

If you think that's a bit fanciful, look at what the eminent psychologist Dr Leonard Kristal had to say on the matter recently.

'Teddies spell comfort and security,' he said. 'They remind grown-ups of the happiest times of their childhood. There's nothing threatening about him—he never yells back! And it's comforting to have something around that's lived with you all your life. And still likes you. There's nothing wrong with teddies for adults!'

This 'closer-than-close' relationship—as it has been called—can start around a child's first birthday, in fact, and in the years which follow, the Teddy Bear will not only be the recipient of all a

Teddy Edward searching for his family tree? The famous little bear photographed by Patrick Matthews.

child's emotions—good and bad—but sometimes may be more 'real' than other live childhood friends.

This bond grows quite naturally, almost unconsciously, and remains a source of comfort throughout life; it is, perhaps, most accurately described by the term 'Bear Awareness'. Apart from celebrating 'The Year of the Teddy Bear', our book looks into this phenomenon and suggests that the power it embodies is actually an inherent characteristic that mankind has possessed since the earliest times. (We also decided to publish the book this year because it marks the 80th anniversary of the start of the 'Teddy Bear Craze'—a fashion which swept America and then Europe in the aftermath of the simultaneous development of the teddy in both America and Germany.

Since the publication of our previous book, *In Praise of Teddy Bears*, in 1980,* we have received scores of letters from people all over the world who are Teddy Bear lovers, asking for more information about their little furry friend. Some of them were very conscious of the influence their teddies had had on their lives, and were happy to share these experiences, while others were still nervous of admitting the fact.

The Teddy Bear Lovers' Book will, we hope, show these people —as well as anyone else, for that matter—that Teddy Bears *can* and *do* influence and enhance people's lives, whatever their age. If you are a sceptic *now*, we very much doubt you will be one by the time you reach the last of these pages.

Philippa and Peter Waring

*Republished in 1984 as *Teddy Bears* by Treasure Press, London.

THE BEARING OF NAMES

A recent survey among 350 children showed that almost 45 per cent of them called their Teddy Bears 'Teddy'. Among the other popular names were 'Ted', 'Brumas', 'Honey', Cuddles', 'Tubby', 'Woolly', 'Curly' and the various ursine heroes such as 'Pooh', 'Rupert', 'Teddy Edward' and 'Paddington'.

There have, however, been some Teddy Bear lovers who have been rather more imaginative in their choice of names for their bears, and so here is a selection of one hundred of the famous (and not so famous) names of bears which we have collected from all around the world, together with those of their friends.

Thread Bear (*Mrs Elsie Chant, England*)
Grand Paw (*Bob Crews, USA*)
Sir Teggy (*Jill Bennett, England*)
Toowoomba (*Dr Barnardo's, Australia*)
Bunga Dingalong (*Herbert Von Caravan, England*)
Bully Bear (*Peter Bull, England*)
Littlejohn (*Mark Steele, New Zealand*)
Ignatz (*Larry Linville, USA*)
Upsi-Duck (*James Tree, England*)
Baron Bear Von Richthoven (*Tony Bastable, England*)
Rufaco (*Eftihia Hobdell, Greece*)
Lionel Theodore Bossyboots (*Wanda Koseda, USA*)
Alexander Graham Bear (*Alan Bialosky, USA*)
Tedkin (*Pamela Scott, South Africa*)
One-Eyed Connolly (*Mrs Helen Walton, New York*)
Jomi Mitshki (*Olga Werner, Germany*)
T. Dan Bear (*Alison Callum, England*)
Terwilliger Beahr (*Jeannie Miller, USA*)

Bully Bear—Teddy Bear power personified!

Chad (*Kenneth Pearson, Canada*)
King Edward Theodosius The First (*Robert Mealy, USA*)
Ivan the Terribear (*Patricia Fitt, USA*)
Teddy Girl (*Colonel Bob Henderson, Scotland*)
Teddy G. Bear (*Gordon Jones, Australia*)
Chinkee Marmaduke (*Ruth Enevoldsen, USA*)
Cosy (*Terry Price, South Africa*)
Maxie (*Mrs Maria Wrist, England*)
Savoyard-Winnistrand-Pooh (*Savoy Hotel, London*)
Theda Beara (*Shirley Kabet, USA*)
Aloisious Ichabod (*Selma Sprouse, USA*)
Burlington Bertie (*Marion Waller, England*)
Collins A.A. Bear (*Jean Collins, USA*)
Dusty (*Jonathan Kramer, USA*)
Humphrey (*Mrs Margaret Thatcher, England*)

A trio of famous International Bears. 1) From South Africa, Mrs Kay Wolfson's bear Cuddle Teddy whom she sketches in her voluminous correspondence with young and old teddy lovers. 2) Leonard Bear from Australia is the mascot of the LEGACY Fund run by Eric Hart. 3) The much-travelled Hans Bear who currently lives with Wanda Loukides in California.

Weinstein (*Marc Stutsky, USA*)
Sunny the Bear (*Angela Bohning, USA*)
Sir Gangy de Brownman (*Mrs Katherine Clarke, England*)
Simon Barsinister (*Patricia Fitt, USA*)
Mr Woppit (*Gina Campbell, England*)
Randolf Caldecott John (*Helen Williams, USA*)
Lambchop Fat Face (*Peter Bull, England*)
Ambidexterous Jones (*James Walt, USA*)
Brownie (*Marie Aspioti, Greece*)
Buddy Bear (*Debbie Ganzel, USA*)
Yardley (*David Gilroy Bevan, England*)
Edward Mode (*Paula Mead, New Zealand*)
Alexander, King of the Royal Alexandrian Kingdom of Small Bears (*Lydia Fillingham, USA*)
Bear-Up Bear (*Paul Hopkins, Canada*)
Fishy (*Sally Kovalchick, USA*)
Barty Blue Bear (*Wanda Koseda, USA*)

Theda Beara, the 'vamp' bear as drawn by her friend Shirley Kabet.

Mr Bear (*Samantha Eggar, England*)
Shadrak (*Betty McDermid, USA*)
Porridge (*Dartmoor Prison, England*)
Ursus Major (*Dorothy Green, USA*)
Clarence Chair-Bear (*The Marquess of Bath, England*)
P. Bearr (*Nicolletta Karam, USA*)
Sinnamon (*Jean Hadley, USA*)
Gilbert Bear (*Yvonne Langley, Australia*)
Theodore (*Peter Bull, England*)
Mr Einstein (*Dusty Springfield, USA*)
Bogie Bear (*Greg Louganis, USA*)
Great Uncle Bushey (*Helena Speed, England*)
Fred Humphrey Tuttle (*Colyn Saal, Australia*)
Lord Neville (*Elizabeth Bentley, USA*)
Thatcher Bear (*Howard Shepherd, England*)
Sleeper (*Peggy Bialosky, USA*)
What-A-Mythe (*David Collins, South Africa*)
Brandy (*Jeannie Miller, USA*)
Sir Tubbs de Squaretoes (*James Walt, USA*)
Brouhaha (*Patricia Fitt, USA*)

Growly (*Colonel Bob Henderson, Scotland*)
Eggie (*Virginia Walker, USA*)
Hunter Bunter Bear (*Peter Bull, England*)
Floppy (*Deirdre Mackinnan, USA*)
Dumper (*Barbara Wolters, USA*)
Theodore Thau Teddy (*Theodore Thau, USA*)
Digger (*Colonel Tom Carhart, USA*)
Juicy Apple Bear (*Jenny George, England*)
Moretonhampstead (*Gahan Wilson, USA*)
Ready Teddy (*Anne Wilson, Australia*)
Ecclesia (*Dorothy Green, USA*)
Arkark (*Bill van Straubenzee, England*)
Oliver Q. Dodger (*Mary Batchelor, England*)
Edward de Bear (*Bonny Carr, New Zealand*)
Bunga-Dingalung (*Olga Werner, Germany*)
Mousey Tongue Bear (*Patricia Fitt, USA*)
Podge (*Osborne Clarke, England*)
Senior Under Officer Edward Bear (*Sandhurst Military College, England*)
Spud (*Scottish Parachute Regiment*)
Lady Elizabeth (*HRH, The Queen Mother*)
Baby Grunt Grunt (*Jenny Hollingsworth, England*)
Major Laing (*Ruth de la Mare, England*)
Biggie (*Pauline Clowes, England*)
Thecupboardwasbear (*Anthony Grimwood, Canada*)
Big Ted & Little Ted (*Patricia Chamberlaine, Australia*)
Pythagoras (*Mabel Evans, USA*)
Teddy Edward (*Patrick Matthews, England*)
Tiglath Pileser (*Sylvia Ffinch, England*)
Sir Edward Bear Bt. (*Elizabeth Rimmer, England*)
Archibald Ormsby-Gore (*Sir John Betjeman, England*)
King of the Cuddlies (*Philippa & Peter Waring*)

Theodore, one of Peter Bull's much-travelled bears.

BEAR THOUGHTS

The Most Memorable Quotes about Teddy Bears

'Growing up without a Teddy Bear is like missing an important link in the chain of events that make up a lifetime. Something like growing up without the love of two parents, or grandparents, not believing in Father Christmas or all those things in Fairy Tales, not even believing in tomorrow and all the things you're going to do with it.'

Shelley Juchartz, collector

'A teddy is soft and warm and inevitably becomes the father figure in the nursery. As people grow older and have to face worries, their teddy becomes the means of recapturing the serenity of childhood.'

Carl Bruin, psychiatrist

'Despite broken growls, noses hanging by the slenderest of threads, worn paws, and the occasional loss of an eye, they remain steadfast and true through thick and thin. They are there when wanted, but quite content to await your pleasure . . . an ideal recipe for the perfect friendship.'

Michael Bond, author

'My Teddy Bear was the very first masculine love in my life.'

Barbara Cartland, 'The Queen of Romantic Fiction'

'Ask your adult friends how many of them still keep a childhood Teddy Bear at the foot of the bed and the numbers will surprise you—*if* they confess, that is.

'And if they don't keep them in the bedroom, their teddies can

'Teddy's Dream'—a superb comic sketch by the great humorist W. Heath Robinson, drawn in 1931.

be found on the lounge furniture or the back seat of the car, the poop deck of the weekend boat, or the office desk.

'Actors and footballers use them as mascots and many confess unashamedly that Teddy is a guiding spirit without whom they would be unable to face the Saturday match or a theatre opening night.'

Richard Edmonds, journalist

'No Teddy Bear lover would ever refer to their little furry friend as "it". For as a number of psychologists have observed, the teddy is a curiously asexual creature, and the choice of whether it be male or female is very much at the discretion of the owner.

'Several bears to our knowledge have wardrobes equally filled with items of little boy's clothes and little girl's dresses, though we rather suspect from their expressions the bears would prefer to remain naked as the creators intended!'

Nursery World, May 1979

'Do you love your Teddy Bear? Do you carry him around with you, talk to him secretly, cuddle him when you're feeling down? Are you 45? Be not ashamed. The day of arctophile liberation is at hand.

'Arctophiles, for those not familiar with ursine lore, are Teddy Bear lovers. The world is full of them. Millions of grown-ups treasure their battered, eyeless, one-eared, furry little friends.'

Vicki Mackenzie, *Women's Weekly*, Australia

'My own progress as an Arctophilist started when I was about seven or so, and my mother asked me what I wanted Father Christmas to bring me. I was quite definite, "A golden Teddy Bear".

'That was a fairly tall order in those years just after the war, for toys were scarce in the shops. Somehow Mother managed it. So my faith in Father Christmas remained untouched, and Golden Teddy came into my life.

'Quite when the last shred of torn, tattered bear was laid to rest, I don't know—in fact, I don't *want* to know. Perhaps he just faded away.

'I *do* know that when I was about 20, my mother actually dared to send him to the local jumble sale—so I naturally stormed right down there and brought him back. You can't fool around with friends like bears.'

Jay Heale, South African Radio, 1981

'A perfectly sensible journalist of my acquaintance went quite berserk recently when she went home for a holiday to discover that her mother had given her squashed and much-loved old teddy a facelift in her absence—even to replacing the little red tongue he'd lost years before.

'In a passion of indignation, the extra stuffing was removed, number two tongue swiftly went the way of the first, and bear and household were restored to their familiar selves.

Susan Roosevelt, the great-grandchild of the American President, with the original 'Teddy's Bear'.

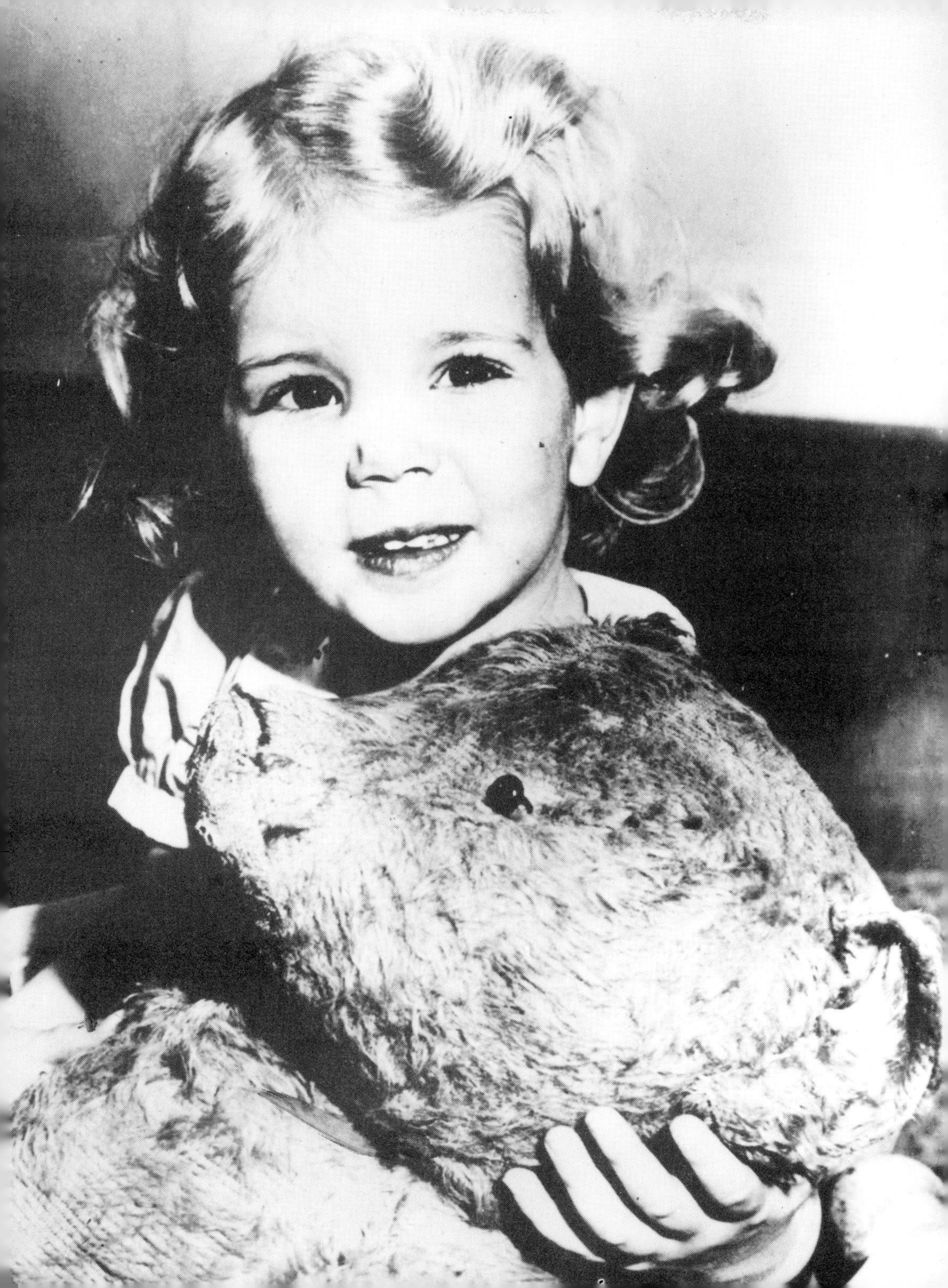

'Indeed, teddies are reputed to have caused family rifts, figured in fierce custody battles and even, poor things, been entombed in the coffins of their owners.

'One young man was distraught enough to write to "Dear Marje" on the *Daily Mirror* because his new bride's teddy had gone along on the honeymoon and severely put him off. His bride, he said, had become hysterical when told their bed wasn't big enough for the three of them. Teddy, it seems, is man enough to inspire jealousy as well as love.'

Anna Baranski, *Family Circle*

'Teddies make scary things manageable.'

Marc Slutsky, Chicago psychiatrist

'Bears are a comforting fortress against anxiety.'

Helen Williams, Rochester, Michigan

'A bear by nature is an extremely ferocious animal, and probably the last creature anyone should really like. Yet, for some reason the bear is probably the most loved of all wild animals—and especially by young children.

'Psychiatrists put it down to the psychological fact that a Teddy Bear is a soft, cuddlesome little chap who simply asks for sympathy from the day he leaves the shop where he has lived since coming from the toy factory. Ordinarily, a bear is terrifying to a child, but when the Teddy Bear comes along, the child who owns it feels that she or he is the little bear's protector by reason of his smallness and cuddlesomeness. With this feeling comes one of assurance. It is as if that child were to say, "Why, a bear is nothing to be afraid of, it comes to me for comfort."

'Of course eventually the bear becomes tattered and torn, with an arm, leg, ear missing or even an eye. It is returned to the nursery shelves, but even then not thrown away, but kept by the owner into adult life. If he or she gets married, more than likely this old Teddy Bear is handed down to their own children.

'Rupert Bear was, of course, a teddy in picture form, but tens of

'No ordinary bear'—Teddy Edward photographed after winning his skiing medal.

thousands of old readers still remember the pleasure he gave them when young. Many indeed still hold firmly to their old Rupert annuals which represent the happiest days of their lives.'

W.O.G. Lofts, Historian and Biographer of Rupert

'Pooh Bear's longevity stems from the stories being passed down from parents who had loved them as children to their own offspring. And, of course, because they are read aloud.'

Christopher Robin Milne, inspirer of the Pooh stories

'Why all this excitement about a Teddy Bear? Well, first of all Teddy Edward is no ordinary bear with his medal which he won skiing, but it is a fact that Teddy Bears have been international characters ever since Teddy Roosevelt, the American President, inspired them.

'Generations of children have had and loved Teddy Bears—there are even clubs like the *Good Bears of the World* of which Teddy Edward is a distinguished member—and there is really no sign that the modern child will ever desert them.'

Patrick and Mollie Matthews, chroniclers of Teddy Edward

'Teddy stands in for the mother who won't let you go out in the snow again; for the father who has just roared at you because your paper boat was made out of today's newspaper; for the aunt who puts you out of the kitchen like a naughty puppy just because you've spilled paint on the floor. One only has to watch children playing with their furry people to see how it goes: they take out on teddy what grown-ups do to them.

'Most mothers have had the shaming experience, in fact, of seeing their own motherhood techniques played out by child and bear. A mother may think she has always behaved in a perfectly Spock-like manner, saying everything in a cheerful, matter-of-fact tone of voice; she may think she has kept a smile on her face and shown unbelievable restraint—until she hears the child saying, "Teddy, will you keep still. Put that back AT ONCE! Teddy, if you don't pick that up this very minute I shall spank you—no, I'm *not* sorry, it was *meant* to hurt, you're a VERY NAUGHTY BOY!"

'All bears are scape-bears; they take the sins of the world upon them.'

Katherine Whitehorn, *Observer* columnist

'So many people remember their early Teddy Bear with such affection, that Grannies will come into our shop looking for one like they treasured when they're buying for their grandchildren.'

Roseanne Wheler, 'Bear Necessities'

'The feverish collecting of Teddy Bears was fanned by the lavish British television production of *Brideshead Revisited* based on Evelyn Waugh's book.

'When actor Anthony Andrews appeared as Sebastian Flyte, lovingly hugging the furry Aloysius, nostalgia seemed ratified by the cultural establishment.

'Devotees have always known that every proper teddy has a mind of his own. Few, though, venture to make the case so directly as Flyte, who orders a silver brush with very stiff bristles—not for grooming, "but to threaten him with a spanking when he is sulky".'

Toronto Star, December 10, 1984

'The cult of the Teddy Bear now has the status of something like a fringe religion. Sometimes 15,000 and more bear enthusiasts turn up at "picnics" to swop stories about their bears and show them off.

'Mrs Thatcher, for instance, has often let Humphrey, her bear, go on show for good causes. So have Princess Anne, Enoch Powell, Derek Nimmo and Lord Bath, whose bear, Clarence, wears spectacles.

'President Reagan, though, said No. He does not lend his Teddy Bear to anyone. And Pope John Paul also prefers to keep his teddy safe in the Vatican rather than let it out for the new craze of international Teddy Bear picnics.'

Ted Gartell, *Sunday Express*, August 1984

'Teddy Bears are the biggest love of my life—after my wife and four children. If all the world leaders had teddies, perhaps they wouldn't be so aggressive!'

David Gilroy Bevan, MP for Yardley, Birmingham

'If you have a Teddy Bear I don't see how you could ever get rid of it. After all, there's no scheme for pensioning off old Teddy Bears!'

Clement Freud, MP for Isle of Ely, Cambridgeshire

'To the extent of not having a Teddy Bear, my early childhood might be described as disadvantaged.'

Richard Nixon, former American President

'I bet if a survey was taken you'd find that all the evil people, the troublemakers in this world, never had a Teddy Bear when they were little children.

'Now if each one of these poor souls were to receive as a gift a teddy, which would be exclusively their own, this would fill in

that missing link in their lives and they would be better people.'
Jane Brown, New York, in a letter to the authors

'The wonderful thing about Teddy Bears is that no one can talk about them without smiling. They just stop any kind of growling!'
Abbie Hatton, Massachusetts Federation of Nursing Homes

'A Teddy Bear is a solacing object—something everybody needs. Do you know that 90 per cent of the sociopaths I have examined never had such objects as children?'
Paul Horton, Connecticut psychiatrist

'Teddy Bears are personalities, each one having his own characteristics, and although our own bear is quite naturally the most precious, we meet others in all walks of life, often taking them for granted and never giving a thought to the stories behind them.'
The Book of Teddy Bears, 1964

'I am writing to say how grateful I am for my lovely teddy, Patrick.

'I love him and I talk to him. Please, sir or madam, I thank you all connected with Good Bears of the World for giving him to me.'
Letter from a Torquay patient to GBW

'Teddy Bears are a comfort against anxiety'—a comment by Time *magazine, 1980.*

'I am a firm believer in the power of the Teddy Bear. Teddies can be rather like father figures to both young and old. To children in particular they represent goodness, benevolence and kindliness.

'In my opinion, any parent who attempts to replace this cosy, unharmful toy is a menace!'

Dr Joshua Bierer, Institute of Social Psychiatry, London

'I have always loved Teddy Bears and have many of them—all sizes, colours and types. I am an artist and also teach art at present to elementary children.

'Quite often I use Teddy Bears for the subject of art lessons. There's nothing like a bear to motivate children!'

Charlene D'Alessio, Stratford, Connecticut

'We feel that Teddy Bears have a definite therapeutic benefit for emotionally disturbed children. In some cases, it's just giving them at the right time which counts so much.

'For example, we gave one to an 11-year-old girl who was just about to have an operation. She hugged it and said, "I don't know what to say." We also gave some to children at a residential clinic in Exeter for emotionally disturbed children. Their immediate reaction was to pick them up and love them, even the tough-looking boys.

'We had a letter from a consulting psychiatrist there saying he hadn't realised how such a small gesture could have such a positive effect. He said the children were also taking them to bed at night.

'Another bear we gave to an old lady whose dog had died. She was too old to take on the responsibility of any more pets. She loved the bear and it became a good talking point with visitors and helped her recover from her grief.'

Jenny George, Good Bears of the World Den Leader

'Thank you for the gorgeous Teddy Bears which we received from you. The two large ones have taken up their new homes—one in the Children's Unit in the Astley Ainslie Ward, and one in the

Unit in Douglas House. The smaller Teddy Bears have gone to our Medical Social Worker's Department, where they will be distributed to children who are obviously deprived of such toys of their own.'

Letter to GBW from the Royal Hospital for Sick Children, Edinburgh

'The comfort and joy that the bears have brought our children is very evident and there is no question that the Teddy Bears helped alleviate any sense of insecurity which they may have felt.'

Richard Davi, Honolulu Children's Hospital, Hawaii

'Airport authorities regularly find evidence that the teddy-troth pledged in childhood is not lightly surrendered.

'The X-ray screen often reveals the plump silhouette with upright ears and outstretched arms, snugly stowed in the hand-luggage of jet-lagged businessmen.'

New York Times, January 25, 1985

'Besides having had a love for bears for years, I have used them as therapy for patients at the Veterans Hospital where I am Chief of Recreation.

'Teddy Bears make excellent prizes for patients. Sometimes they are kept for personal enjoyment, and sometimes given to others as a gesture of warmth and friendship. Giving them as prizes covers up, for many, the embarrassment of going out and buying one for oneself.

'I feel a person who can openly show affection for a Teddy Bear is really better equipped to relate with others than those who scoff or deny a liking.'

Dick Stracke, Lorena, Texas

'There's nothing childish about Teddy Bears! They are no more childish than collecting wives, cars or yachts.

'And think what they can do for you! The average bear doesn't mind being taken for a walk, dressed in ridiculous hats or even

Teddy as a soft, cuddly playfellow—from the Sears, Roebuck Catalogue, 1926.

being read to. You can also blame him for anything and he won't deny it.

'Adults have a definite and equal need for the dear creatures. There is a vast underground Teddy Bear movement.

'We arctophiles are a touchy lot, and insults or ridicule by ignorant persons puts our hackles up. One is Teddy Bear conscious in the same way other people are car, garden, clothes, food or cat conscious.'

Peter Bull, 'The Teddy Bears' Champion'

'Arctophiles are people obsessed with Teddy Bears and they are better organised than you might think. They all share a feeling for their Teddy Bears comparable to Citizen Kane's for Rosebud the sled.'

Sunday Telegraph, April 22, 1979

'Teddies are an important emotional part of a kid's growing up, a security item. Sometimes mommies and daddies are too busy to listen. Teddy Bears are *never* too busy.'

Andrew Morrison, to *Time* magazine, June 11, 1979

'Teddies go everywhere and do everything. There is not a corner of the globe that they have not penetrated. Their appeal is universal and to all ages.

'They have gone into battle on guns, tanks and haversacks; saved lives by intercepting bullets; flown all over the world in aeroplanes; been "drowned" in floods, burned in concentration camps and worshipped as Totems; used extensively in advertising campaigns; collected by film stars, ballerinas and actresses; used as mascots and talismans; had endless books, songs and verses written about them; are taken to hospital, are indeed part of our everyday life—and all within the space of a few years.

'It is also not always realised that a Teddy Bear is not just a Teddy Bear—the varieties are absolutely endless, one sort being more suited to a certain age group or type of owner than another.'

Margaret Hutchings, author, 1964

'True enthusiasts say a bear's real value is in the holding. Threadbear remnants from childhood have climbed mountains, accompanied RAF pilots into the Battle of Britain and shared foxholes in Vietnam. Cookery expert George Villiers credited "Rupert" with saving his family when they escaped from Nazi-occupied Norway. Drifting in the North Sea, the bear waved to a British reconnaissance plane, and convinced the crew that the family was British.'

Newsweek, December 24, 1984

'My own love of bears, particularly one, is lifelong. I received "Growl" for Christmas in 1950 and he slept with me until I was married in 1970. Needless to say he is now quite frail, almost without fur, and his growl no longer works. But he is beautiful.

'Growl knows more about me than anyone else. He listened to me through all the crises of growing up. Should I ever lose him, I think I should feel I had lost all of my childhood, as well as my oldest friend. I do think everyone should have such a companion as Growl.'

Kathy Snell, arctophile

'My Teddy Bear is something like God except everyone has God and only I have my Teddy Bear. Teddy doesn't take the place of God. It's just that God knows I am weak and need something material to love and trust in. I think he makes me easier to live with. Instead of having my emotions bottled up inside me, I tell Teddy my sorrows and together we work out a solution. I think he is one of God's most wonderful creations.'

From a letter to Peter Bull, 1968

The Teddy Bear as mascot.

'Each year the Teddy Bear is becoming more widely recognised as a silent symbol of love and understanding, so needed in the world today. Teddy Bears bring smiles, ease loneliness, provide consolation and unite people in friendship. They function as symbols of peace and happiness universally.

'The Teddy Bear acts *in loco parentis* as an archetypal mother/father understander-of-all. It is society's comforter.'

Colonel Bob Henderson, Good Bears of the World

'The philosophical idea that Teddy Bears are more than a stuffed toy, but rather part of today's society, was in evidence at the Longleat Rally in 1979. Historic as that event was, our bear consciousness tells us that this is only the beginning . . .'

Jim Ownby, Good Bears of the World

'During the last 75 years, Teddy has become a friend to millions of boys and girls and untold numbers of adults.

'For generations of children left alone in the dark he has been the guardian who kept watch while they slept. He has never said a word, but by his presence alone has dispelled fears and given encouragement.

'Probably no creature or creation in history has done so much by doing so little. Teddy is now famous, not so much for what he *is*, but for what children over these 75 years have given him. As bedroom companion and friend, giving undivided attention at all times, he has generated a faith that lasts a lifetime.

'Neither President nor seamstress, toymaker nor toy store, gave him that. A child did; and a child-like mind still does, for to be a genuine arctophile is an adult appreciation, not a childish trait.'

Bear Tracks, Spring 1979

BEAR WITH US

People in all walks of life love Teddy Bears. Some of the most famous people in the world today still cherish their faithful old friends from childhood—just as do uncounted thousands of ordinary men and women. Indeed, it makes no difference whether you're rich or poor, distinguished or just plain average; teddy can have precisely the same effect on you. And it's something no one need be the slightest bit embarrassed about.

Take Prince Charles, who will one day be King of England. He still has a very soft spot for 'Teddy', a now somewhat battered golden bear he was given by his mother, the Queen, when he was an infant more than thirty-five years ago. This beguiling old chap was never far from the Prince's side during his childhood, and even accompanied him when he went to prep school at Cheam and later to Gordonstoun.

One of Prince Charles' favourite tunes is 'The Teddy Bears' Picnic', and there is a delightful story told of how, on one of his birthdays when he was still at prep school, he requested that the Grenadier Guards play the tune for him and 'Teddy'!

The Prince's bear now resides in his home, Kensington Palace, keeping affectionate company with another, smaller, golden bear which belongs to his charming wife, the Princess of Wales. Because they are both teddy lovers, they have given bears to their two children, Prince William and Prince Harry, and both boys have shown similar affection for their furry friends. (When they were born, the youngsters were also presented by members of the public with quite a large number of Teddy Bears, but as the Prince and Princess felt it would be impossible to keep all these, the majority were generously given to charity.)

World leaders are similarly smitten with 'bear awareness'. The British Prime Minister, Mrs Margaret Thatcher, has a splendid chap named Humphrey who has been with her since childhood. He has become something of a politician, too, and has accompanied Mrs T. on a number of her election campaigns. He spends much of the year quietly in Number 10 Downing Street, but with his owner's permission is an enthusiastic attender at charity-raising functions where he is invariably the centre of attention.

The slightly put-out look some friends thought they observed in April 1979 was subsequently explained. Humphrey had been left behind when Mrs Thatcher made a tour of the Labour marginal seat of Paddington and instead was accompanied on her tour by a young fellow called Paddington Bear!

The Pope also possesses a small bear which has been with him since his youth in Poland and now lives in some dignity in the Vatican in Rome. Unlike Humphrey, however, this bear is not permitted public appearances. The same goes for Ted, the bear belonging to the American President, Ronald Reagan, who is one of the original bears inspired by President Theodore Roosevelt.

In fact, virtually every US President has followed in the Roosevelt tradition by owning a Teddy Bear, and particularly fine specimens have belonged to the recent incumbents John F. Kennedy and Lyndon Johnson. Only the unfortunate Richard Nixon did *not* have a bear when he was a child . . .

The British Houses of Parliament contain a number of teddy lovers whom we happen to know personally because a number of them came to the launching party for our previous book, *In Praise of Teddy Bears*, which was held in the House of Commons. Foremost among these is David Gilroy Bevan, the MP for Yardley, Birmingham, who has a 'hug' of sixteen bears including a fine specimen called Yardley—for obvious reasons! Mr Bevan has, in fact, founded a Den (or group) of bear lovers in the House, among whom can be numbered Enoch Powell, Clement Freud, Eric Heffer, Sheila Faith and Sir George Young.

There are plenty of teddy lovers among the nobility, too, with the Marquess of Bath and his friend, the distinguished, bespectacled Clarence Chair-Bear at the very forefront of these. It was the Marquess who, by holding the famous 'Teddy Bear Rally' at his home, Longleat in Wiltshire, in June 1979, first really made the world aware of just how widely teddies are collected and loved.

For the two days of that bank holiday weekend, teds of all shapes and sizes, from all over the world, were on parade. Some were in their owners' arms or in their pockets; others came in haversacks and shopping baskets, or in prams, pushchairs and trolley bags. There were as many bears in the arms of adults as children, and there was no doubt that, for those 24 hours, Teddy Bears ruled OK.

Lord Bath was certainly amazed and delighted at the gathering. 'Everyone joined together in a companionship that was quite extraordinary in its simplicity,' he said. 'It was totally removed from the pressures that the modern world puts upon us. I found it so heart-warming—the teds and their families all seemed to have *such* a happy time.'

The Marquess received lots of comments about Clarence, and he confided to one national newspaper reporter, 'Although,

The Teddy Bear MPs gather in their 'Den'—or to be more precise, the House of Commons!

Clarence Chair-Bear with Lord and Lady Bath and some of their other teddies.

unlike me, Teddy Bears abhor publicity, for worthy causes they can overcome their distaste.' (In this instance, the event was raising money for disabled people.)

Lady Bath also has a teddy—and one with something of a history. The bear was given to her almost sixty years ago by the famous singer Gracie Fields who was a close friend of her mother. Today the teddy has been worn almost completely smooth by hugging, and so rather prefers to appear in public in a jacket or coat.

'He's a dear—and such a good friend,' says Lady Bath.

Apart from the Prince and Princess of Wales, several other members of the Royal Family still cherish their childhood bears. The Queen Mother, for instance, has a lovely old brown bear, Lady Elizabeth, and Princess Margaret still looks after the little fellow her father, King George VI, gave her during the Second World War, to comfort her during the bombing raids on London.

Princess Michael of Kent is devoted to her old friend, and

Princess Anne's son, Master Peter Phillips, has regularly been seen in public with his honey-brown bear under his arm.

There is another Royal story that nearly had a sad ending. On a tour of the Far East in 1961, Princess Alexandra lost her teddy which had accompanied her. Despite exhaustive swoops by RAF aircraft over the Irrawaddy where the little bear had last been seen—as well as many forays into the jungle by the Burmese Army—he seemed lost forever. Then, miraculously, he turned up in a *laundry basket* after the Princess had returned to England. Thanks to an obliging jet pilot, the two were soon reunited!

Members of the acting and media professions are also great Teddy Bear lovers. Take Selina Scott, host of the BBC TV *Breakfast Time* programme. For years she regarded her childhood teddy as a lucky charm which had helped her reach the top in her profession. But when a charity close to her heart appealed for gifts to raise money, she handed over the bear in a most touching gesture. Immediately, though, she was given a replacement, which she jokingly named Frankie, 'because he reminds me of my co-presenter, Frank Bough!'

The late star of the TV series *Crossroads*, Noele Gordon, was for years one of the most excellent ambassadors for Teddy Bears. Her home at Handsworth Wood was almost full of bears that she had been given by fans, and she was always ready to promote the cause of the bear.

'Isn't it funny,' she once told *TV Times*, 'as a child you take teddies seriously. And as an adult you feel loath merely to dismiss them as toys. I know I do; I take my teddy very seriously. I've met human beings who didn't have *half* the personality he has.'

One TV star who actually owes his success to a Teddy Bear is the ventriloquist Roger de Courcey. His foil is an amazing bug-eyed Cockney teddy called Nookie who, as everyone who has seen Roger's act will know, is a saucy little rascal. Roger is in no doubt as to what this bear has done for him.

'I was just a stand-up comic and singer before I found Nookie,' he says. 'He was the one who really got me started. We met in 1970 at a jumble sale in a Scout Hall in Stoney Stanton in

Leicestershire. I had arrived early in the town to give an evening performance, and so to kill some time I wandered around the sale.

'On one of the stalls I found this battered old Teddy Bear. I started fooling around with him, and some of the people nearby began to laugh. So I bought the bear—he cost me five pence, I remember!—and developed the idea further. At first, I just used the ted for a throw-away line in the middle of the act. But gradually he took over. I called him Nookie—and thanks to him I've gone from a Ford Escort to a Rolls Royce.'

Roger adds reflectively, 'I suppose it was really a case of Nookie discovering me! I certainly believe in him when I'm working, but I don't talk to him unless I'm performing or rehearsing. If audiences ever stop looking at Nookie and start looking at me, I'm in trouble. I know my lips move, but it doesn't bother me. Some ventriloquists are technically perfect, but not necessarily funny. What is important is that Nookie is the star.'

Generous praise indeed from a man who has undoubtedly experienced a striking case of 'Teddy Bear Power'! Over the years, incidentally, Roger has worn out ten models of Nookie. But the original chap that put him on the road to fame and fortune is still around, enjoying a very well-earned retirement at his home.

Among other entertainers who have lovingly kept their teddies can be listed Derek Nimmo, Judi Dench, Penelope Keith, Esther Rantzen, Michael Aspel, David Dimbleby, Kenneth Kendall, Faith Brown, Simon Le Bon, Mary Parkinson, Cilla Black and Su Pollard.

Actress Jill Bennett has, however, a slightly ambivalent attitude to her teddy called Sir Teggy.

'I've had him longer than I've been alive,' she says. 'My mother bought him in Penang two weeks before I was born. He is bolshie, vile, unpleasant, fascist and I hate him, but if I don't take him everywhere he'll never forgive me. He's even got earrings now and gone all poofy!'

Naturalist and author Gerald Durrell, who goes to some of the farthest corners of the world, actually only got his first teddy recently—when he was married. It was given to him as a wedding present by his wife, Lee, in May 1979, and has been an inseparable companion ever since.

Among other notables who have allowed their teddies to make public appearances for charity are the explorer John Blashford Snell, the 'Queen of Romantic Fiction' Barbara Cartland, cartoonist Roland Emitt, and that one-man cricket team, Ian Botham.

America, too, boasts an aristocracy of Teddy Bears. The Kennedy family have retained several of their life-long furry friends, as have the Rockefellers and Gettys. In Hollywood, producer John Schlesinger has a bear imposing enough to direct any film, while actor Elliott Gould is widely considered the film capital's most famous teddy lover.

He revealed recently that he has three bears who like to act out the morning and evening television shows. Elliott is, though, rather concerned about any publicity for his Teddy Bears because, he says, he 'rather fears for their peace of mind in the hot-house atmosphere of Hollywood.'

Shirley Temple, the child star turned politician, was well-known for appearing in her pictures with teddies, and still retains her affection for them today, as do Bette Davis, Lauren Bacall and Shirley MacLaine.

The TV show 'M*A*S*H', which only recently came off the air after years of success, boasted two Teddy Bear lovers, Larry Linville, who played Frank, and Garry Burghoff, who was the effervescent Radar O'Reilly. Larry, who sadly lost his own childhood bear, Ignazt, when he was getting divorced, is so attracted to teddies that he spends his spare time making them for sale in a store run by his sister-in-law and called very appropriately, 'Bear 'N' Grin It'.

Garry Burghoff, on the other hand, still has his battered old childhood bear, and it was recently used as the model for 'Radar's Teddy', a distinctive-looking chap who is now being sold throughout the country to benefit the Paralysed Veterans of America charity.

Shirley Temple, Hollywood's best known teddy lover.

Elvis Presley, the great Teddy Bear fan, on the film set of Love Me Tender *with two co-stars and the friend he called Bear'd Dog.*

However, America's most famous showbiz teddy lover of recent years was undoubtedly the late singer Elvis Presley—who also owned the biggest collection of bears. Elvis had actually owned a teddy since his childhood, and this ragged little friend was never far away right through his youth and after he became a sensational world star in 1956 with his record 'Heartbreak Hotel'.

Not surprisingly, when a couple of American song writers named Kal Mann and Bernie Lowe heard about Elvis' love of teddies, they composed a special song which they felt sure would go down well with the fans. It was called 'Teddy Bear'—or to give it its full title, 'Let Me Be Your Teddy Bear'. It was a cute, cuddly song, like its subject, and Elvis recorded it with obvious feeling in Hollywood in February 1957. The song was also featured in the film *Loving You*, made that same year, Elvis' second movie in which he played Deke Rivers, a character very much like himself who rises from being a poor truck driver to a singing star.

Fans did indeed love the song, and within days of its release in June 1957, Elvis found himself being deluged with gifts of teddies. A few weeks later his home was packed with little furry friends and it was difficult to find room for any more. Generously, Elvis gave many of them away to local hospitals and children's charities, although certain favourites he retained for his personal collection. No count has ever been made of just how many bears Elvis was given—although one estimate has put it as high as eight thousand!

Of all these teddy lovers, one man and his bear remain perhaps more famous than any others: the late Poet Laureate, Sir John Betjeman, and his friend, Archibald Ormsby-Gore, the inspiration for one of the finest poems in the English language, *Summoned by Bells*, and less directly the inspirer of a character in Evelyn Waugh's classic novel, *Brideshead Revisited*. For the sight of Sir John carrying this bear about with him while he was a student at Oxford, gave Waugh, who was also there, the basis for his character Lord Sebastian Flyte and his inseparable Teddy Bear, Aloysius. (When this book was so successfully adapted for television in 1981, it was not Archie who filled the role, however—Sir John would not hear of such a thing—but one of Peter Bull's bears, who became a star overnight. Of which more later in the section, 'The Torchbearers'.)

Although Archie undoubtedly relished his fine-sounding name, he had almost literally been hugged to death in his seventy-odd years of life. His once golden fur remained only on his back, and as well as several patches, his eyes were made from wool and his ears and nose were pieces of cloth. Just over a foot tall, he preferred to sit sedately in Sir John's London home, where he was once described by his friend as 'very protestant looking'.

Archie was always a courteous host to other bears who visited him and Sir John, and he was certainly secretly proud of having inspired those moving lines in *Summoned by Bells* (published in 1960) which referred to him as 'my safe old bear . . . whose ample forehead I could wet with tears'. Sir John's description of how he would sit and wait for hours to see him move, 'convinced that he could breathe', are surely among the most evocative ever written about a Teddy Bear and without doubt capture the very essence of bear affection.

Nor does Archie's fame end there. For Sir John also wrote about some of his later adventures in a delightful story called *Archie and the Strict Baptists* which was published in 1977. This provided the clue to the origin of Archie's name—it came from one of the music hall tunes sung by the great comedian George Robey—and also revealed the little bear's strong religious convictions. Sir John once elaborated on this.

'Archie has a very strong personality and I rather regard him as my conscience,' he said. 'He has strict Baptist principals, and strongly disapproves of smoking and drinking. I do, too.

'Archie also spends a great deal of his time contemplating the futility of mankind and the Last Judgement which he believes only the Strict Baptists will survive.'

The story of Archie was written by Sir John when he and his family lived in the historic old town of Uffington in Berkshire; it describes the little bear's investigations into local history (he is

Sir John Betjeman's own sketch of his famous and much loved bear, Archibald Ormsby-Gore.

convinced that molehills are the graves of baby druids) and tells how he made himself a pair of wings from brown paper so that he could fly to meetings of the local Strict Baptists (shades of hang gliding there!). Sir John gave us a copy of one of the sketches he made of Archie which the artist Philida Gili utilised for her pictures to illustrate the story—and it is reprinted here.

Because of his religious beliefs, Archie had a terror of publicity and absolutely refused to be photographed when the Poet Laureate celebrated his 70th birthday in 1976. He was, though, a constant source of support to his friend during his busy years as a writer, poet and campaigner on behalf of historic buildings and monuments. Sir John felt that if he could pass on just a little of the warmth and comfort he had received from Archie he would be well rewarded.

The special bond between these two was movingly demonstrated in October, 1983, when Sir John suffered a heart attack and had to be rushed to hospital. When Archie was later hurried along to join him, the hospital staff reported that the patient 'rallied remarkably'. This example of teddy power in hospital was appropriately recorded in some verses by one of Sir John's friends, the poet Gavin Ewart. He wrote:

There's a breathless hush over Crescent and Square
and the Gardens are sad and still
while everybody, yes, everywhere, wonders: Will
Sir John go over the Hill?

The agonised cry goes up: Rush that bear
to his grieving, tormented side!
This is the comfort, in his despair, far and wide
All wish for him, tearful-eyed!

This is the single much-more-than-toy
That can succour him in his need—
Archibald, seventy years of joy,
of joy indeed,
As Venerable as Bede!

So take him by taxi, by tube or by train,
Fly him so high in the air!
Give us some hope, let us breathe again
(oh, if we dare!)
and speedily RUSH THAT BEAR!

Sir John, of course, recovered from this heart attack, and he and Archie returned once more to the peace and seclusion of their home. The patched and much-loved little fellow was also by his friend's side when the wonderful old man died a year later. In their obituary of Sir John, *The Times* very appropriately referred to him as 'a kind of Teddy Bear to the nation'.

There was not a dry eye—human or *ursine*—in our house when this sad news reached us . . .

BEAROLOGY

A Chronological listing
of the important Paw-Marks
in the Teddy Bear's History

Mid-Nineteenth Century. The first models of bears made from soft fabrics as distinct from wood, metal or carved stone are produced in Europe. In Russia, the Brown Bear has been a traditional toy among children for centuries, generally called 'Mishka'. At this same period, English children knew the cubby-bear as 'Bruin' in much the same way that 'Bunny' was used for rabbit, 'Dobbin' for horse and 'Pussy' for cat.

August 9, 1902. King Edward VII is crowned in Westminster Abbey, and because of his love of bears and his nick-name of 'Teddy', some people have claimed *him* as the inspirer of the name Teddy Bear.

November 14, 1902. While on a bear hunt on the Mississippi Delta, the American President, Theodore Roosevelt, is offered the chance to shoot a cornered bear. He refuses to kill the ageing animal.

November 16, 1902. President Roosevelt's humanitarian action receives widespread publicity, and the political cartoonist of *The Washington Post*, Clifford K. Berryman, immortalises the event in a sketch which portrays the bear as a delightful little cub.

November 20, 1902. Morris Michtom, the owner of a New York novelty shop, is so taken by Berryman's cartoon that he has his wife make some plush fur models of 'Teddy's Bear' which create immediate interest among his customers.

Spring 1903. At the Leipzig toy fair in Germany, an American buyer from F.A.O. Schwartz is shown a small soft toy called 'Bear' made by the firm of Margarete Steiff in Giengen. He is so

(Left) *President Theodore Roosevelt, the man who gave his name to the Teddy Bear, calmly watching two bears feeding while on a bear hunt.* (Right) *Morris Michtom.*

impressed he places an immediate order for 3,000 for the following Christmas.

Christmas 1903. Having received President Roosevelt's permission to use the name 'Teddy's Bear' on his honey-coloured plush bears, Morris Michtom begins to distribute them widely through the New York wholesalers, Butler Brothers.

Spring 1904. The generic name of both the German and American manufactured bears has now become 'Teddy Bears', and the astute President Roosevelt capitalises on their rapidly-growing popularity with the US public by using several models in his campaign for re-election. His success gives an early indication of the appeal of the bear.

Summer 1905. America goes 'Teddy Bear mad'. Demand for the bears has mushroomed all over the country, and suppliers are hard-put to keep pace with the 'Teddy Bear Craze', as the Press call it.

Spring 1906. The craze begins to spread far beyond the bounds of America, although in the USA the interest in the bears has

(Left) *Margarete Steiff.* (Right) *President Roosevelt with his four sons, photographed in 1904, shortly after 'Teddy's Bear' was born.*

already confirmed that it is more than a child's toy. Reports a New York journalist, 'Teddy is all the rage in the cities. The children carry him to school and even the grown-up ladies carry him with them when they go out for a walk or ride, or go to the theatre.'

April 1907. First publication of the most famous of all teddy melodies, 'The Teddy Bears' Picnic'. Composed by John W. Bratton, the catchy tune is to remain without its now-familiar words until 1930 when the British lyricist Jimmy Kennedy pens the immortal lines. This tune has proved to be the first of an almost uncountable number of songs to feature the Teddy Bear.

The first 'Teddy's Bear'—a model on exhibition in the Smithsonian Museum, Washington.

A rare 1903 Steiff bear like this one would be worth well over £1,000 today if it were in equally good condition.

Autumn 1908. Other American manufacturers, anxious to find a rival to the Teddy Bear, promote toy possums—and although the initial interest is high, the craze proves short-lived. The Teddy Bear is King!

November 1908. The first all-British Teddy Bear is launched in London by Dean's Rag Book Company, heretofore publishers of 'untearable' books for infants. Their set of three bears, Mother and her cubs, Teddy and Sissy, are an immediate success, and Dean's have continued at the forefront of the market ever since.

Summer 1910. The craze for Teddy Bears has caught on in Britain and Europe, too. A newspaper reporter comments, 'Society women in Edwardian England clasp nothing to their bosoms with more devotion than their teddies.' By the time the 'Twenties have arrived, no fashionable drawing-room is without its bear, and leaders of society like Syrie Maugham have all-white teddies perched in positions of honour on their blanched Chippendale settees.

November 8, 1920. First appearance in the *Daily Express* newspaper of Rupert, destined to become the longest living strip cartoon character. Created by Mary Tourtel, he is in time to be referred to as 'The Mickey Mouse of Great Britain'.

March 1924. Walt Disney introduces the first Teddy Bear in colour on the cinema screen in his version of 'Alice and the Three Bears'.

September 1926. First appearance of the immortal Winnie-the-Pooh. Created by the playwright and humourist, A.A. Milne, the little bear is based on a real teddy that belonged to his son, Christopher Robin, who is also featured in the stories.

Autumn 1939. Teddy Bears become inseparable companions of many people caught up in the terrible Second World War. Children and adults find comfort from the relationships with their bears, and the multitude of stories which come to hand would almost certainly fill a book. As *Time* magazine reported later, 'Teddies flew as wartime mascots in Spitfire cockpits, and also went into battle perched on guns, tanks and ships.'

April 1951. Russell A. McLean, having become convinced of the Teddy Bear's ability to cheer up children in hospital, begins to raise funds to make gifts to little patients in the two hospitals in his native Lima, Ohio. The example of Mr McLean, who is nick-named 'The Teddy Bear Man', soon spreads widely . . .

Spring 1962. Lieutenant-Colonel T. R. 'Bob' Henderson, a former British Army officer who retired in 1955, and has been researching into the influence of the Teddy Bear on Western Society, is nominated President of the Teddy Bear Club.

The authoress and her teddy after a German air-raid on England during the Second World War.

December 1967. The first major survey of Teddy Bears is conducted by *Which* magazine. The investigative journal begins its five-page report: 'In recent years, some sinister Teddy Bears have been found with unhealthy insides which might well harm their owners in the latters' more carnivorous moments.' The magazine has carried out 'post mortems' on 40 British bears, and concludes, 'By and large, we can give British Teddy Bears a clean bill of health. There was very little wrong with the great majority.'

October 1969. Publication of *Bear with Me*, the first book devoted to the Teddy Bear, written by the devoted collector and well-known actor, Peter Bull. It generates an enormous amount of correspondence for Peter, and makes him aware of a whole 'underground movement' of Teddy Bear lovers all over the world.

October 27, 1969. Jim Ownby, an American journalist and charity worker, who has been deeply impressed by Peter Bull's book, founds the Good Bears of the World organisation, appropriately in the Swiss 'bear town' of Berne. The day is chosen specifically because it marks President Roosevelt's birthday. The group is registered as an international humanitarian society dedicated to presenting Teddy Bears to sick children and adults, as well as uniting arctophiles (Teddy Bear lovers) in friendship and benevolent activities all over the world. Current membership of GBW stands at 8,000 members in the USA, and over 700 in Britain, with 'Dens' being created throughout Europe and the rest of the world. As a matter of record, GBW now reckons to hand out something like 100,000 teddies world-wide every year.

October 27, 1973. GBW is officially inaugurated with a special function at the Bellevue Palace Hotel in Berne. A reporter says of the occasion, 'The appeal of the Teddy Bear is universal. It is an international symbol of friendship and goodwill, and a bringer of comfort and affection in times of stress.'

November 1974. The prestigious *National Geographic* devotes a special feature to the appeal of the Teddy Bear. 'In greater numbers than ever this winter,' the report says, 'bears are back in the woods—Teddy Bears lying in wait beneath Christmas trees ready to conquer youngsters' hearts. Through the years, they may have been better at it than any other Christmas toy. Countless ancestors of this year's Teddy Bears have been killed with kindness, smothered with love that may cost them a chewed ear, or unbuttoned eye, or a wrenched shoulder seam.' And the feature ends, 'The Teddy Bear is the King of stuffed beasts and all other toys.'

November 1978. The status of the Teddy Bear is confirmed when the toy is portrayed for the first time on a Swedish postage stamp. In America, at the Smithsonian Institution in Washington, a special exhibition is opened in the National Museum of History and Technology; on display is one of the original bears made by Morris Michtom and presented to President Roosevelt in 1903.

November 12, 1978. A special Children's Festival at Leicester Cathedral is attended by an astonishing 1,300 people and over 630 Teddy Bears are donated for presentation to sick children. It is a sign of things to come . . .

May 27, 1979. The seventy-fifth anniversary of the Teddy Bear is marked with a spectacular 'Great Teddy Bear Rally' at Lord Bath's stately home, Longleat House in Wiltshire. Over 18,000 people attend from all over the world, complete with thousands of Teddy Bears. 'It wasn't so much a revolution, as a revelation,' says Colonel Bob Henderson. 'It was the beginning of the Teddy Bear Front.' This view is shared by Colin Randall of the *Daily*

The symbol of the Great Teddy Bear Rally at Longleat in 1979.

Telegraph, who writes, 'The world's most prolific and popular variety of bear, the cuddly Teddy, received its glorification in the clinging Wiltshire mud.' And Richard North of *The Observer* adds, 'It was the greatest congregation of stuffed bears the world has ever known.' The rally is the first of its kind—as well as being the biggest Teddy Bears' Picnic anyone has seen—and at last all the world is made aware of bear affection . . .

August 23, 1979. New Zealand follows the lead of Longleat with their first Teddy Bear Convention held in St Luke's Square, Mount Albert, Auckland. Over 500 Teddy Bears attend with twice that many human friends to take part in a variety of competitions, games and displays.

August 27, 1979. Not to be outdone, Australia stages its first Teddy Bear Rally in Bankstown Square, Sydney, from August 28 to September 8. Thousands attend the gathering which raises money for the widows and children of ex-servicemen, and a highlight is the display of more than 260 Teddy Bears collected from all over the world by Mr and Mrs Don Talbot. (This collection now forms a permanent Museum open daily in Brisbane, containing 500 exhibits at the last count!)

October 23, 1980. 'National Bear Awareness Week'. To promote 'bear awareness' in Britain, a happy week of parties, exhibitions, rallies and Press features is organised. Our first book, *In Praise of Teddy Bears* is published, and the day is marked by a special launching party in the Houses of Parliament attended by members of the Westminster 'Den', complete with their bears, and led by the Marquess of Bath and David Gilroy Bevan, MP for Yardley, Birmingham. Money is also raised for GBW and, speaking of the charity, Mr Bevan says, 'It is well worth leaving the cut and thrust of parliament for a short while to help children who are sick.'

August 30, 1981. 'Bears' Bank Holiday' is held at Longleat from August 30 to September 6, attracting in excess of 40,000 people and their bears. Among the highlights are a display of bears belonging to famous people and a number of special events, all of which causes one visitor to declare, 'It was a deluge of teddies of every description!' Pam Goodger, the Public Relations Officer at Longleat, adds, 'There's no doubt the "Bear's Bank Holiday" could have lasted for a month!'

June 4, 1982. The first major American Teddy Bear rally takes place in Philadelphia Zoo, Pennsylvania, attracting more than 25,000 people as well as countless bears. A variety of stalls and booths cater to every bear's needs, and experts are on hand to help people date older bears as well as repair those in need of attention. A delighted Jim Ownby of GBW says afterwards, 'The Good Bear trail grows longer, wider and more colourful as we spread through all the nations of the world.'

July 1982. Teddy Bear fever again sweeps America. According to the *New York Times*, 'It is the summer of the Teddy Bears. They are everywhere. In Bloomingdale's in New York they dominate the new wedding department, and carrying one is, apparently, an invitation for a cuddle. And Aloysius, the star of the hottest new television series, *Brideshead Revisited*, is in demand everywhere for guest appearances . . . The underworld of Teddy Bear lovers are surely out of the closet!'

December 29, 1984. After an ever-increasing number of rallies, as well as further widespread publicity about the appeal of Teddy Bears, *Newsweek* magazine devotes four pages of its Christmas issue to the phenomenon. 'It may be the era of electronic whizbangs,' the magazine declares, 'but some of the best-selling software these days is Teddy Bears. US sales, about $40 million a year in the 1970s, swelled to $125 million last year, and retailers think next Christmas (1985) will be the biggest bear market ever. More than 40 per cent of sales are *to* adults and *for* adults.' Why should this be, *Newsweek* asks Elena Diaz, chief toy buyer for Marshall Field & Co. 'Bears mean escapism, whimsy and fun,' she replies, 'and nobody's too old for that!'

January 2, 1985. 'The Year of the Teddy Bear' begins. According to a report in *The Times*, the Teddy Bear epitomises carefree childhood and has been chosen as the perfect symbol for UNICEF's Year of Youth which is just beginning. Manufacturers are aiming to make the Teddy Bear the most in-demand item for Christmas stockings, says the newspaper, adding 'This is the year the bear will supplant the Cabbage Patch dolls.' As part of the festivities to mark this special year, a 'Teddy Bears' Concert' is held at the Barbican Centre in London.

April 9, 1985. So successful was the concert at the Barbican, that a second event is held by public demand. The 'Bearly Barbican Baroque Teddy Bears' Concert' is again packed out by youngsters and their furry friends. Fraser Goulding conducts the London Concert Orchestra and TV star Ian Lavender acts as compère. This same Easter Monday, a Teddy Bears' Picnic is held at Harewood House, Leeds, and generates such interest that BBC Radio 1 broadcasts an hour and a half live show from there, introduced by Mike Read and Peter Powell.

June 13, 1985. The start of the 'International Teddy Bear Tour', with a parade through the streets of London (via Buckingham Palace) of a convoy of thirty small C5 motor vehicles driven by 'Teddy Bears'. A picnic is held in Kensington Square attended by many famous bears, to raise money for the Save the Children Fund. During the tour, from June 17 to August 26, picnics are also to be held at 15 locations including Alton Towers, Staffordshire; Botanic Gardens, Belfast; Strathclyde Park, Motherwell; Pontcanna Fields, Cardiff; and a grand finale at Longleat on August Bank Holiday Monday. Organised by the International Teddy Bear Club in conjunction with Save The Children, the tour features exhibitions of teddies, displays by parachuting bears and a competition to find 'The Teddy Bear of the Year' . . .

And the future? 'Bear awareness' is surely only just *beginning* to exert its tremendous appeal . . .

THE SECRET OF BEAR AWARENESS

The expression 'bear aware' was first coined in the autumn of 1980 to help promote our book, *In Praise of Teddy Bears.* The idea was to present a week of special events for Teddy Bear lovers of all ages—including picnics, parties and displays of bears—to highlight the extraordinary appeal of teddies. It was called 'National Bear Awareness Week' and proved a tremendous success.

'The response was amazing,' one of the organisers told us later. 'People everywhere were so keen on the initial idea—and it just grew from there.'

It grew so quickly, in fact, that special events mushroomed all over the place and the book's sales far exceeded the initial expectations. Indeed, a little while later, the London evening newspaper, *The New Standard*, was noting:

'Books on collecting always seem to do well, but the surprise success this year seems to be a volume about jolly Teddy Bears. Arctophiles have united to buy over 15,000 copies of Philippa and Peter Waring's *In Praise of Teddy Bears . . .*'

Now, while it would be very ego-boosting to claim that we started something new, the fact is that 'bear awareness' has been around for a very long time indeed. The man who knows more about it—and has devoted more time to investigating it—than anyone else is Colonel Bob Henderson, arctophile *par excellence* and himself the owner of a huge 'hug' of bears. He it was who introduced us to the hobby of collecting bears (called arctophily and derived from the Greek words *arktos* meaning bear and *philos* for friend or lover). Every model bear can tell a story, he says, linked with some person, place or thing. Teddy Bears in particular

'No other toy seems to have the healing effect of the Teddy Bear'—Colonel Bob Henderson.

are mementoes of love, friendship, happiness and security, and collecting them is a most enjoyable pastime offering the pleasure of the search and the satisfaction of new discoveries. As you might guess, Colonel Bob's fascination with things Teddy Bear is all-engrossing, and his dedication in promoting an understanding of the deeper meanings is quite tireless.

'Each year,' he says, 'the Teddy Bear is becoming more widely recognised as a silent symbol of love and understanding, so needed in the world today. Teddy Bears bring smiles, ease loneliness, provide consolation and unite people in friendship. They function as symbols of peace and happiness universally.

'Doctors have told me,' he goes on, 'that teddies help a child to settle down in hospital and recover more quickly. No other toy seems to have this healing effect to such a degree and we need to find out more about this power. Indeed, it's one of the most interesting psychological problems of our time . . .'

The origins of mankind's fascination with the bear can, in fact, be traced to the very earliest times, as even the most perfunctory study of folklore, legends and even fairy tales will show. These clearly indicate that the bear has always been widely regarded as a representative of both divine and natural forces; and they show why today, in the form of a Teddy Bear, it is grasped in psychic compensation and clung to for security.

'The reason for this,' explains Colonel Bob,' is that the bear functions as a powerful symbol that provides satisfaction for a widespread psychological need. Consequently, history, religion, philosophy and psychology are all involved in any proper explanation of the mystique of the Teddy Bear.'

Undoubtedly mankind has always felt there was something mysterious about the bear, and the worship of these animals goes back to the very dawn of time. The famous British zoologist Dr Desmond Morris has suggested that our fascination with bears may be due partly to their ability to stand upright on their hind legs like us—and as they are manlike, powerful and ferocious, yet can also look warm and cuddly, this could well explain the origin of bear-worship.

Certain it is that Neandertal man, about 100,000 years ago, carefully placed the skulls of bears on special stone slabs like altars. Such skulls, found in Drachenloch in Switzerland and near Nuremburg in West Germany, were of giant cave-bears. And although these animals were vegetarians, they were sufficiently large and brawny for those ancient people to believe they were gods.

Neandertal men also demonstrated what are widely believed to have been the very earliest forms of religious expression, when they performed a 'rite of intensification' to seek power from the bear god. They built a model of a bear complete with bearskin and a bear's head, into which they plunged spears in the hope of acquiring the animal's power when they went out hunting for food. In these large representations can be seen the prototype of the model which has today become the Teddy Bear. Neolithic figurines dating from as far back as 6500 BC also show goddesses wearing bear masks.

With the passing centuries, bear worship developed all over the world. In Japan, for instance, at least 10,000 years ago, the Ainu people would take the body of any wild bear that had been killed to the nearest settlement and roast and eat it. During the eating, however, it would be worshipped with songs and prayers. (Interestingly, the Ainu people still exist in remote areas of Japan today—*and* continue their reverence of the bear.)

The North American Indians are, of course, the people most associated with bear worship. Certain tribes—including some branches of the Apaches—would never even touch a dead bear, let alone kill one. The Cherokees, Mikes and Iroquois were among those Indians who prayed to 'bear spirits' and also held 'bear dances' in which the creature's movements were imitated. In many tribes the medicine men would wear a costume resembling a bear. Some Indians even gave their children small models symbolising the bear gods, these infants thereby becoming the first to play with a 'toy' bear!

Bear worship was similarly evident in ancient Greece and Rome. In Greek mythology the seven-starred constellation we know as *Ursa Major*, or the Great Bear, was originally named *Arktos* after the she-bear. It was the Romans who changed it to *Ursa Major*, as they believed it represented the goddess *Artemis* whose animal form in art was a bear.

In virtually all the bear cults there was a great fascination with the animal's ability to hibernate, and this became closely associated in a symbolic way with mankind's absorption with death and resurrection. Consequently bears became linked with humans in legends about the Creation.

For centuries, there was an idea that a bear gave birth to its young in an unformed mass and then 'licked' it into shape. Man took up this idea by referring to his own offspring as 'cubs' who also needed 'licking into shape'. A 'Bear Leader' likewise became the term for an adult placed in charge of a young person who needed advice and guidance in order to develop to maturity. The parallels grow ever closer, you see . . .

Over the years other attributes were ascribed to the bear which were firmly held, but which can now be seen as superstition. For example, in the sixteenth century it was believed that the grease of a bear prevented baldness, while if you rubbed it on your garden tools it would prevent plants from becoming diseased.

According to an old superstition, the bear 'licked' its cubs into shape from an unformed mass, as this twelfth-century illustration shows.

Well into the nineteenth century it was said that any child who rode on a bear's back would be automatically immunised against whooping cough, and it is still held in parts of Europe and America that sleeping on a bearskin rug is a cure for backache, and that a bear's tooth is a lucky charm against toothache!

In Europe today, there is still evidence of bear worship of the old kind. In certain villages and small towns in Southern France each Spring, for instance, a man will dress up in a bear costume and pretend to go to sleep in a mock 'cave' specially built in the centre of the community. Then he will wake up, leave the cave and for half an hour or so 'prowl' around frightening the local inhabitants. This is the focal point of what is called the 'Bear Festival' and it continues with dancing and feasting.

The town of Berne in Switzerland is, of course, the place most connected with the bear. The coat of arms displays a bear, and it is said that the town got its name in the twelfth century when the founder, Duke Berchtold V, decided to call it after the first animal he killed in a hunt. Later, in the year 1480, the city opened a bear pit, and the animals have been on show in the deep pit near the Nydegg Bridge ever since.

The twelve or so bears in residence there are well-looked after and beautifully cared for, and the regular arrival of new cubs around Easter time has proved a never failing delight to the locals, as well as countless millions of tourists. Not surprisingly, because of their long association with bears, the Bernese have erected statues of them in the streets and on churches and public buildings. And, apart from being fond of the creatures, they rather resemble them, too, as an official Berne tourist office hand-out agrees:

> Many writers have mentioned the intimate connection and similarity between the bear and the Bernese. The common physical traits are very striking: thick-set, bull-necked, broad-chested, with long dangling arms, great hands and powerful legs, the Bernese has the same nonchalant walk as the bear—or is it the bear which imitates the gait of his human brother? In character, too, bear and Bernese resemble each other. Awkward and somewhat grumpy, they dislike their toes being trodden on and their habits being interfered with, but are easily appeased by friendly treatment, which acts as a balm to their pride and makes them draw in their claws.

From all these historical facts, it is therefore very evident that there is much about the bear that appeals to mankind—and much in its nature that forms a bond between us.

The city of Berne features a bear on its coat of arms.

The idea that the images and symbols of mythology can be transmitted to present-day man via modern archetypes is one that has been developed by the Swiss psychiatrist Carl Gustave Jung, the brilliant pupil of Freud. The basic principles had been explored long ago by ancient writers such as Pliny and Plutarch, but it is primarily through Jung's work that the ancient power of the bear can be aligned with the influence of the Teddy Bear.

Carl Jung established his reputation with his work, *Theory of Psycho-Analysis*, published in 1912. In this work, he advanced the idea that apart from the personal unconscious, there is a 'collective unconscious' which, at the very deepest level, all humans share. In this 'collective unconscious', he said, resides all human experience, and specific images—which he called archetypes—arise from it and form the basis of the human psyche. The image can be an inherited symbol, and it is our belief that 'bear awareness' comes about as a result of mankind's enduring link with the bear since prehistoric times. In a nutshell, the archetypal bear in the 'collective unconscious' finds its latest expression through the Teddy Bear.

Jung also maintained that these archetypes seem to possess a power and energy of their own, directing, inspiring and moving a person in a particular way. Colonel Bob Henderson has explained this particularly vividly.

'Such "effect" images can rarely be reduced to words,' he says, 'they are "experiences" and speak for themselves, as do works of art and rituals. For example, you don't ask what a dance means—you enjoy it. In just the same way, you don't ask what teddy means—you enjoy him. The experience the Teddy Bear gives you is like a dance with the spirit of a play.

'Yes, he is a toy, a bear-doll. But he is also at the same time an "effect image", a mystic symbol, something transcendental, an instrument of inner communication or communion. That is why the Teddy Bear so often takes on a personality and seems to be very much alive—a "living doll". Everybody captivated by his charisma "dances for joy" at the life-furthering influence he generates.'

Because the idea of the bear is so deep-seated in the human soul, Colonel Bob says, it is easy to see why the phenomenon of Teddy Bear consciousness lies largely in the subconscious plane of the mind and is not readily appreciated. The awareness does, however, seem to be strong in small children—although not exclusively so, as another arctophile, the distinguished writer, Eithne Wilkins, wrote in 1975:

> This phenomenon is, in fact, so intense, so widespread, and so utterly taken for granted by adults—many of whom adhere to it themselves—that the bear in the form of the Teddy Bear has, oddly it seems, become our society's comforter. That almost all-pervading cuddly creature, which for so many children is more important than any doll, and which remains with so many adults as something at once intrinsic and marginal to their most intimate life, acts *in loco parentis* as an archetypal/mother/father/understander-of-all.
>
> This is because we not only need comfort, but guidance also. In religious symbolism the Great Bear, from whom we take our bearings, has provided this; and the form of the bear, as represented by the Teddy Bear, has become our comforter. Comfort lies in mystery, for closeness also lies in mystery, and both lie somewhere in the absolute. This ultimately accounts for the fantastic appeal of the Teddy Bear, which derives from the absolute function of the symbolic bear, its function as a surrogate for the mother as comforter, and for the Holy Ghost as The Comforter.

Such statements establish the Teddy Bear as far more than a simple toy; indeed it is credited with psychotherapeutic powers by a number of medical people, including Dr Traude Motzko, an Austrian who believes teddies can establish a state within the human mind and body which is beneficial to healing.

'I believe the Teddy Bear can form a link with the old symbols of love and affection,' she explains. 'And the greatest symbol behind it is surely one of kindness and strength, and therefore of safety and shelter, providing a sense of security and protection beyond measure.'

These qualities, it is said, are what can make a teddy of such value in hospital to the ailing young and old alike, and of such comfort to the dispirited and lonely.

Colonel Bob believes that 'bear awareness' is still in the process of being revealed, and he plans to continue investigating the phenomenon through Good Bears of the World, of which he is the United Kingdom leader. Similar investigative work is being done by Dr Paul C. Horton of Chicago University, who believes that the progressive use of transitional objects such as the Teddy Bear into adolescence and adulthood can culminate in mystical experience.

In the final analysis, however, it still seems that the greatest joy to be reaped from being 'bear aware' is the childhood memories it can bring back, for surely the very shape, feel and even smell of Teddy Bears is associated with the memories of love, friendship, happiness and security upon which childhood is built? And such emotions are essential to the peace of mind we all seek.

Enquiries may well be opening our minds to certain special qualities which are inherent in the Teddy Bear; but it is in each individual relationship with a bear that the real key lies, and that is something so personal that there are really no words to describe it. Nor, perhaps, are any really needed.

THE TORCHBEARERS

The fact that the whole world is becoming 'bear aware' owes a lot to three men who have put the Teddy Bear's case to the public and proved that there's not the slightest need to be worried about loving your teddy—whatever age you may be; in fact your life can be a lot more fun as a result. These men, are the redoubtable Lieutenant-Colonel Henderson, the ebullient and much lamented actor, Peter Bull, and the industrious American arctophile, Jim Ownby.

'Colonel Bob', as he is affectionately known to his many friends around the world, both human and ursine, is a tall, white-haired, immensely likeable man who looks every inch the soldier he was for much of his life. With his courteous manner and immaculate moustache he usually strikes people meeting him for the first time as the most unlikely person to have campaigned on the Teddy Bear's behalf. Yet he has brought the same military efficiency to organising the Good Bears of the World group in Britain that he once did as a regular army officer with the Royal Scots Guards. Colonel Bob lives in a typical grey-stone house in Edinburgh. Typical, that is, until you go inside: for spread throughout the house's numerous rooms is the most remarkable assembly of teddies you could wish to see—almost 600 of them; including both true Teddy Bears and models of bears collected from all over the world. This splendid array gazes at you from shelves, mantelpieces and the tops of tables, while a great many more are ensconced in chairs and almost defy the visitor to move them!

Pride of place among this impressive 'hug' of bears undoubtedly belongs to Teddy Girl, surely one of the most

Colonel Bob Henderson with his close friend and source of inspiration, Teddy Girl.

appealing Teddy Bears still in existence. She is beyond question the oldest and best-preserved teddy in this country, and is also unique in having undergone (if you'll pardon the expression) a sex change! She it is who graces the cover of this book, and also inspired the little drawing at the start of each chapter. That she has a personality all her own is immediately evident when you meet her—indeed those dark, inscrutable yet warm eyes seem to sum you up as soon as you meet her—and also follow you around the room wherever you go. This distinguished bear has been in Colonel Bob's family since he was a child, and having been made in 1903 is certainly one of the very earliest examples. There is a delightful portrait of Teddy Girl with the young Bob Henderson and his brother, which enjoys a prominent position in the house.

Colonel Bob shared the bear—then considered a male—with his brother throughout their childhood. When the elder Henderson lost interest in the teddy, Robert kept him as the basis of his collection, and through him came to appreciate the special position a Teddy Bear can have in a child's life; he understood why many of them remain the treasured possessions of their owners throughout the rest of their lives. Colonel Bob chose the Army as his career, and by the time of the Second

World War was a lieutenant-colonel. He served with distinction on General Montgomery's staff and kept a little teddy with him the whole time, even during the gruelling fighting across the deserts of Africa.

'He was a miniature bear,' Colonel Bob remembers fondly. 'I kept him in my ruck-sack and he went absolutely everywhere with me. He was my link with home and happiness. I got a great deal of comfort from him and he helped me get through. Unfortunately, though, he didn't survive the war, getting so dusty he literally fell to pieces.'

In 1955 Colonel Bob retired from the Army and began to investigate in earnest the phenomenon he calls 'Teddy Bear Consciousness', which we refer to as being 'bear aware'. His research took him into many fields of investigation not previously covered adequately by others because, he says, of their fear of derision. It was only when he started what he called the 'Teddy Bear Club' in 1962 that he began to persuade arctophiles to overcome their timidity and admit the feelings they had for their little furry companions.

'The evidence that then became available was a complete revelation to many people,' explains Colonel Bob. 'It became evident that the phenomenon of 'Teddy Bear Consciousness' was practically inherent in the human psyche. The 'Teddy Bear Club' was therefore something much more subtle than a cult. It did, however, from time to time come into conscious existence and practical activity at various places all over the world.'

This 'practical activity' took the form of the organisation Good Bears of the World which is dedicated to bringing Teddy Bear lovers together, as well as to raising money to bring comfort to those of all ages in the form of gifts of Teddy Bears.

Colonel Bob's inspiration in much of his work has been provided by Teddy Girl who, he explains, was given 'her' sex-change by his daughter, Cynthia, who took to the venerable dark-brown bear with the same affection that her father had done. For years the little girl and the teddy with its deep growl were inseparable. Then, one fateful day, the re-named Teddy Girl was left at home by her young mistress when she returned to school, taking with her two new additions to her Teddy Bear family.

The frilly-skirted bear sat disconsolately on her mistress's bed all that term, Colonel Bob remembers. And when Cynthia returned home, a very odd change had come over the old teddy. She refused to growl when given an affectionate squeeze of welcome; and she has not made a sound from that day to this!

Thinking about Teddy Girl's story, one can imagine *what* tales she might tell if she chose to talk! Such, though, has not been the case with Peter Bull or his two most famous teddies, the tiny Theodore and the television star, Aloysius. His death in 1984 robbed the world of arctophiles of a good friend and sturdy champion whose TV appearances and book, *Bear with Me*, published in 1969, did much to unite teddy lovers everywhere.

A portly and ruddy-complexioned man who often played haughty or aggressive roles in films or on television, Peter was in fact a kindly and amusing person wholely devoted to his collection of Teddy Bears and ever ready to defend himself and fellow arctophiles. He was always prepared to admit that there were those who thought the very idea of talking or writing about Teddy Bears was enough to 'bring up the bile', but he would work equally determinedly to prove them wrong. On television interview programmes, in which he was invariably accompanied by one or other of the members of his 'hug' of bears, he would delight his host—and the viewing audience—with anecdotes about his little friends. These appearances brought comfort to a lot of people who had felt embarrassed about admitting they were still devoted to their teddies.

Peter could be equally enthusiastic when talking privately in his comfortable flat in King's Road, Chelsea, in south-west London. Surrounded by his collection of over 250 teddies—many of them gifts from admirers all over the world who had asked him (or Theodore) to take care of them as their owners were no longer in a position to do so—he was delighted to regale visitors with stories about bears.

IN PRAISE O
TEDDY BEA
by
Phillippa & Peter War
ELEBRATION IN WO
D PICTURES OF TH
RLD'S BEST-LOVE
CUDDLY TOY
Souvenir Press

Peter devoted many pages to little Theodore in his own book, so there is no point in reiterating that story here; but what he did *not* mention—and, sadly, fate has now decreed that he will never be able to do so—is how he became so attached to Teddy Bears, or the events which turned the hitherto reticent Aloysius into a world-famous star when he appeared in the splendid television version of *Brideshead Revisited.*

Like so many of us, Peter became a Teddy Bear lover in his childhood and, as too often happens, suffered the terrible trauma of having his teddy given away by an unfeeling parent. Indeed, all his life he felt the pain of returning home from school when he was sixteen to find his beloved teddy had been given by his mother to a jumble sale.

'You know, many people have written to me over the years about their traumatic experiences when their Teddy Bears were taken from them as children,' he told us in conversation. 'You must never do that!' he added, well aware that we were the parents of three children. We couldn't help thinking that Peter looked rather like a large, amiable Teddy Bear himself!

His ready wit was a feature of all his public appearances, in which he talked about his attachment to teddies.

'They're so much cheaper than a psychiatrist,' he once told a somewhat bemused David Frost, 'and not nearly so supercilious.'

'Englishmen are far more ready than Americans to confess that they cling to their bears,' he said, somewhat tongue-in-cheek, to radio interviewer, Pete Murray. 'Over there they tend to think that any such sentimentality is a reflection on their virility.'

And he delighted viewers watching the BBC TV programme *Collectors' World* in 1970 by describing how he carried at least three small teddies with him wherever he went, and often gave tea parties at smart hotels especially for Teddy Bears and their friends. 'I have often thought of organising an international bear lovers' rally in the Albert Hall,' he beamed. 'Think how much quieter it would be than Cruft's!'

The ebullient Peter Bull with Aloysius.

He also recounted a story of how two of his bears nearly got him into trouble.

'I was travelling to New York,' he explained, 'and when I got on board the aircraft I asked the air hostess if she would mind fastening the seat belt of my travelling companions—two large teddy bears. Well, she nearly had a fit! She rushed off to the captain convinced they must be stuffed with revolvers and that I was a hijacker!'

But all the stories of Peter's bears pale in comparison with that of Aloysius, who found overnight fame as the constant companion of the eccentric Lord Sebastian Flyte, played by Anthony Andrews, in Granada's acclaimed TV version of *Brideshead Revisited.* However, he very nearly didn't get this part, Peter told us.

'When the dramatisation of the story was being prepared, no one had really thought about casting the bear,' he said. 'But when filming began at Castle Howard, the Yorkshire country house on which Evelyn Waugh based Brideshead Castle in his book, the owner, George Howard, offered his own family teddy, known affectionately as Big Teddy, for the series. Unfortunately, he didn't look appealing enough—the producer, Derek Granger, wanted a larger, more ruffled bear. At this, enter Aloysius.'

In fact, Peter's old friend was just one of six teddies auditioned for the part, but the 74-year-old veteran proved irresistible to both director and actor. He was promptly hired, and at Peter's insistence insured for £1,000 against 'bodily injury or bear-napping'! There were some rather heated exchanges between Peter and Derek Granger, however, when Aloysius was referred to in correspondence as a 'prop'.

'I made it part of the agreement that in all contracts he was referred to as "the artist" and not "the property",' recalled Peter. He later learned that Derek Granger had sent out a memo to his production crew: 'I think it better if the bear were not informed that he is designated a "property".'

Further surprises occurred when filming of the series was suddenly held up by a technicians' strike.

'Of course Aloysius joined the workers on the picket lines,' said Peter. 'But I soon got a bit concerned and wrote to Derek Granger. "Where and how is he?" I enquired. "How much longer will he be employed and is he going to get a bonus for staying with you for so long? He tells me he is not even getting the bear minimum and offers are pouring in here for his services."'

Peter was duly assured that Aloysius was, in fact, being well taken care of. But a little later he had to write to Granada once more.

'I said I needed him back for a show I was doing shortly,' Peter said. 'But I got back a reply that changed everything. They said the artist was just off to Venice with Lord Olivier to shoot some important scenes. What *could* I say?'

Derek Granger himself recalls working with Aloysius on *Brideshead Revisited* in the most affectionate terms.

'The bear was an absolute marvel,' he says. 'Among our older players, Aloysius was marvellous. He was never late on the set, he never bumped into the other actors and was never drunk.

'In actual fact, he continued to work when he was quite ill. At one stage during the 21 months of filming he bled a little straw and had to be rushed off to a dolls' hospital.'

When Aloysius at last returned home, Peter Bull found he now had a star on his hands.

'Even before the series was broadcast and became such a hit, people were getting in touch with me to borrow Aloysius for use in commercials and promotions,' he remembered. 'Suddenly I found myself the agent of a star who could command £35 a day for modelling jobs, plus meals and transport.'

It was a far cry indeed from the days when Aloysius—then rather strangely (though appropriately) called Delicatessen—had languished for almost sixty years on the back shelf of a delicatessen store in the small American town of Saco in the state of Maine. This was a story known to only a few people until Peter revealed it to us.

'Talk about actors having to survive in obscurity before hitting the big time!' he exclaimed. 'Poor Aloysius, who is one of the

Ideal Toy Company's earliest teddies, dating from 1907, just sat about in that deli for 60 years until he was rescued by Mrs Euphemia Ladd, and then emigrated to Britain to come and live with me. Of course, when he got his big chance, I felt it only right to change his name—via a suitable announcement in *The Times*!'

The success which greeted the remarkable bear's screen appearances caused Peter to open a bank account for him, as well as making his will. But he could not get him an entry in the 'bible' of the acting profession, *Spotlight.* 'I can't see why they refused him,' Peter said. 'After all, he is a better actor than most of the people who *are* in it!'

Aloysius' fame was ensured without this entry, however. His picture appeared on the front cover of *TV Times* and *Vogue* magazine, and he was also directly responsible for generating 'an even greater interest in the collecting of Teddy Bears,' as the prestigious American newspaper, *The New York Herald Tribune*, reported in its issue of December 12, 1984.

Peter, though, was not resting on his—or Aloysius'—laurels, and was at this time busy planning to promote another of his teddies, Bully Bear, through a series of amusing little books he was writing. He was already well along with *Bully Bear Goes to a Wedding* (about the little chap being present at the marriage of Prince Charles and Lady Diana Spencer) and *Bully Bear and the Teddy Bear Rally*, which conjured up all the fun and excitement of the famous Longleat gathering in June 1979.

When the two books were published, Bully, through Peter Bull, sent us nicely inscribed copies. It was the final gift we were to receive from a delightful man.

The sketch and message we received from Bully Bear.

The third person who has done much to make people 'bear aware' is the American, Jim Ownby, the founder of Good Bears of the World. That he should have become fascinated with Teddy Bears comes as no surprise when you learn that his middle name is Theodore and that he is a distant relative of the man who began it all, President 'Teddy' Roosevelt! What, though, inspired him to create the Good Bears organisation was coming across a copy of Peter Bull's book *Bear With Me.*

Jim, who is a journalist, broadcaster and public relations consultant, is rather like a big, comfortable bear himself, and he certainly exudes goodwill, kindness and a love of all things small and lonely. It was remembering his own much treasured childhood teddy while he was reading Peter's book about bears and the warmth they can give to the young and old, which gave him his big inspiration.

'That's what started me on the idea of people around the world expressing love and caring by making gifts of Teddy Bears to children,' he says. 'There is something endlessly appealing about the soft, cuddly little figure. So I decided to set up Good Bears of the World, a non-profit-making voluntary association dedicated to bringing together Teddy Bear lovers in America and the rest of the world to raise money to give this lovable toy to children in hospital. For if you're sick and lonely in a strange hospital bed, love *is* a Teddy Bear.'

Jim Ownby actually founded the organisation, most appropriately, in Berne in 1973, but the headquarters have since been moved to Hawaii. He reckoned then that there were somewhere in the region of 170 million Teddy Bear fans in the USA alone, along with more than 500 million bears—so there was plenty of scope for Good Bears!

Since 1973 GBW has developed into a whole series of smaller groups, or 'dens', as they are called. 'Any group in any community can set up their own den, raise funds to buy bears or even make their own,' says Jim. 'They then have the pleasure of delivering them to children in hospitals and seeing the joy they bring.'

Today the organisation has several thousand members in dens

all across America, and similar groups are to be found in Canada, Great Britain, France, Germany, Norway, Australia, New Zealand, and even Hong Kong and Korea. The kind of people who belong to GBW range across the whole social spectrum, and although ages and occupations vary, the 'Good Bearos'—as Jim likes to call members—all share the same fondness for bears as a symbol of affection. They also see teddies as persons rather than things.

According to Jim, GBW members greet each other with 'bear hugs' and sometimes their meetings tend to become 'show and tell' gatherings. For example, one Honolulu woman, back from a trip to her home town in Iowa, displayed the 40 year-old ted she had found in the attic, while another presented 'Chief Bearo' Jim with a bright pink teddy she had bought in Thailand to be added to the GBW museum which contains examples from all over the world. There are also innumerable cases of members' good deeds—like the man who takes teddies to entertain mental patients and another who provides hand-made bears for stroke victims. The list is almost endless.

Recently a professor of educational psychology in America had this to say of GBW: 'I think of the Teddy Bear as a symbol of affection. This is the feeling I sense among Good Bear members. A warmth and human concern for others.'

The GBW badge.

The chief 'Good Bearo', Jim Ownby, the founder of Good Bears of the World.

And a leading Canadian newspaper, the *Toronto Star*, was similarly enthusiastic about the activities of GBW, when Jim Ownby paid a visit there recently.

'The whole idea is such a simple one and so easy to pursue, I can hear the odd disclaimer harrumphing loud harrumphs,' wrote columnist Lotta Dempsey. '"Teddy Bears! At a time when the whole globe seems in such a mess!" Exactly. Any avenue of love and understanding, especially where our children are concerned, is a glint of sun through dark clouds.

'And if you think Jim Ownby is a lonely and slightly daft piper playing his Teddy Bear song to an unheeding audience, hear this . . . It would be impossible to estimate the thousands of bears of every size, shape and texture that have been distributed. In several areas of the United States residents of homes for the aged and those in senior citizen organisations have entered happily into the bear-making volunteer effort.'

GBW has its own delightful newsletter, *Bear Tracks*, and Jim has established October 27—President Roosevelt's birthday—as the annual 'Good Bear Day'. Naturally enough, it's celebrated with picnics . . .

The whole movement is one that deserves success, for, as can be seen, it is putting the very basic ideas of 'bear awareness' to good use. And as Jim Ownby himself says, 'Teddy Bear power is not only love for children and seniors, but for anyone who can appreciate the ideals we have for the Good Bears of the World.'

Long may it continue!

'THE TEDDY BEAR CRAZE'

In turning back the pages of Teddy Bear history, it is fascinating to discover that the credit for giving us this remarkable little chap who becomes our indispensable friend in childhood and loving companion in adulthood, actually belongs not to one but *two* people who had virtually the same idea at the same time, but were separated by the width of the Atlantic Ocean. And it is particularly appropriate to look back to that important period just now, for it was eighty years ago, in 1906, that what has come to be known as the 'Teddy Bear Craze' began.

The story of how a dear little invalid German lady and an enterprising American shopkeeper (who also, curiously, had originated from the other side of the Atlantic, in Russia) created the first true Teddy Bears, has already been told, but the basic details are well worth repeating, particularly as some points are still disputed. Let us take the little lady first, as she was certainly the first of the two to realise the comfort a teddy might provide for its owner. And how did she reach this conclusion which is now seen to lie at the very heart of 'bear awareness'? Because she, too, found comfort and inspiration from a little bear she kept by her side, which had been taken from the very first hug of teddies she made.

Margarete Steiff (pronounced Shtyff) might well have lived a frustrated and unhappy life. Born in 1847 in Giengen-an-der-Brenz, in the heart of the Black Forest region of Germany, she was a bright and lively child until she was two years old. Then polio struck her down, and for the rest of her life she was confined to a wheelchair. For the child of a poor builder this was a terrible blow—what sort of life could she hope for? Only when Margarete

Margarete Steiff and one of the Teddy Bears that made her world-famous.

realised that fate had not robbed her of the use of her hands did she see a possible future, for seamstresses were always in demand; so she set about teaching herself how to handle a needle and thread.

As she grew older, Margarete turned her cottage into a little workshop, and there she stitched petticoats, coats and felt table covers. She particularly liked working on children's clothes—all the more so when the youngsters came along to see her. She had a natural ability as a storyteller, and soon her young customers were less interested in what she was doing than in getting her to tell them a story. And what tales she could weave!

Margarete enjoyed trundling along the forest lanes around her home, and more often than not she would have a little group of children accompanying her, usually clamouring for stories about the animals that lived in that part of Germany—rabbits, foxes, wolves and such like. On one special day, a bright-eyed little girl chirped up:

'Auntie Margarete (for she was "Auntie" to everyone), the animals always run away. Couldn't you make us some to keep?'

The plump little lady's jolly, deep-set eyes twinkled. What a good idea, she thought.

'What sort of animals would you like, children?' she asked.

'A fox,' shouted a boy.

'A wolf,' cried another.

'No, no. A dear little bunny rabbit,' piped up a girl in a pretty print frock.

'Children, children!' Margarete Steiff stilled the clamour with a wave of her hand. 'I will make a toy for *each* of you. Now think carefully, and you can tell me what you would like when the walk is over.'

It was that simple request that set Margarete Steiff on the path to creating the very first teddies. For the little animals which she subsequently made from felt and woodshavings were such a success with the children, that others of their friends came knocking at her door begging for toys. She had found a second string to her bow, and soon the demand for felt toys began to outgrow the calls on her services as a seamstress. Such, indeed, became the demand that she started employing other women in the village to make the toys; their fame spread from village to village throughout the Black Forest, and then into the German hinterland beyond. A contemporary report describes what happened next.

> At first the toys which Margarete made were given as gifts to children who came to visit her. But as demand for them grew, her brother Fritz realised there was a business potential in them and carted a sackful off to the country fair. In a short time all were sold, and Margarete's hobby was put on a paying basis. From this point (1880) until the year 1897, a small family business turned into a thriving industry.

The little house in Giengen where the Steiff Teddy Bears were born.

In 1897, however, after completing his art studies in England and Germany, Margarete's nephew, Richard, joined the firm. While studying in Germany, he had spent many hours sketching the playful brown bear cubs at Stuttgart's famous zoo. These sketches he showed to his aunt as a possible addition to her range.

It was to prove the moment of destiny for Margarete Steiff. She was captivated by the pictures, and immediately set to work creating a new animal. Instead of the smooth felt she normally used, she selected plush or 'fuzzy' brown mohair. She also decided that the legs, arms and head of the bear should be movable, thus creating the very first stuffed toy to have moving joints. She gave the toy a long pointed snout and black shoe-button eyes; it was a creation of sheer genius, as time was to prove—although not immediately, as another German report tells us:

A rare photograph of Margarete Steiff making teddies in her workshop.

Strangely, no one thought kindly enough of the new toy even to give it a name. It was simply 'Bear'.

'Bear' got off to a poor start. At the next Leipzig fair, the Steiff nephews did not even bother to display him. So 'Bear' lay in a packing case, in real danger of meeting an untimely death before the children of the world could pass judgement on him.

The fair was in its last day, however, when an American buyer asked the Steiff nephews if they had anything new. Without much conviction, they pulled 'Bear' out of his hiding place. 'I'll take 3,000,' said the buyer at once. (This perceptive man was a representative of F.A.O. Schwartz, who can therefore claim the distinction of having first introduced the toy to the United States.)

Margarete Steiff was overjoyed at the news. Something inside her had told her this toy was special; and certainly her little friends who had first viewed 'Bear' shared this enthusiasm. Thereafter a model of 'Bear' stood on her desk, while each day she would personally check every duplicate before it left the workshops. A journalist, C.H. Norton, who visited the Steiff works a few years later in 1908, was particularly impressed by this aspect of the operation.

'Every day,' he wrote, 'Fräulein Steiff moves among her workers with a kindly word for each, attending to her business faithfully and above all devoting scrupulous care to the enormous task of personally examining every toy made in her factory. As a safeguard to dealers and the public, a little metal button is firmly attached in the left ear of each animal after it has been examined by Fräulein Steiff, and no animal with this badge of quality has ever been found to have even a slight defect—which bears ample testimony to the earnestness with which the owner does her part of the work in the factory.' (The button has, of course, continued to be placed in the ear of every Steiff bear to this day!)

* * *

A 1907 American advertisement for Steiff bears.

While Margarete Steiff undoubtedly created 'Bear', the world's first soft toy in the shape of a bear, it was the Russian immigrant living in New York, a man called Morris Michtom, who first modelled 'Teddy's Bear'—which, with the deletion of a single letter, became the immortal Teddy Bear. This side of the story was explained by Herbert R. Collins, the Curator of Political History at the famous Smithsonian Institution in Washington. Mr Collins, who has extensively researched the background story of the Teddy Bear, actually staged a one-case exhibition in the National Museum of History and Technology in 1978. Called 'Teddy and the Bear', the exhibit had one real star attraction—the original teddy made for President Theodore Roosevelt. But to begin at the beginning . . .

According to the most widely held version of the 'birth' of the Teddy Bear, this came about as a direct result of an incident in November 1902 when the then President, Theodore Roosevelt, was out bear hunting in Mississippi. After an unsuccessful day, some of the men on the hunt, who were anxious to please the President, captured a small bear which had been abandoned by its mother and brought it to him on the end of a rope. The great man

Clifford Berryman's famous cartoon from the Washington Post *of November 16, 1902.*

BIRTH OF THE TEDDY BEAR (1902)

took one look at the pathetic little creature and replied that there was no way he would kill something so helpless.

This humanitarian act was later reported in the newspapers, and the incident so caught the imagination of Clifford K. Berryman, the political cartoonist of the *Washington Post*, that he used it as the basis for a poignant little cartoon. This sketch was, in turn, seen by a New York shopkeeper who was touched by the President's action and made a small model of the bear which he nick-named 'Teddy's Bear' and placed in his shop-window as a means of catching public attention. Within moments—so the story goes—a man had walked into the store which belonged to Mr Morris Michtom and offered to buy the model bear. The 'Teddy Bear' had thus been born . . .

Such is the oft-repeated version of the legend. The facts, however, are somewhat different.

It is certainly true that President Roosevelt was on a hunting trip in November 1902 and that he did refuse to kill a bear. But the bear was actually a huge old creature that had been found by the hunting party entangled in a mass of ropes. Nor was the animal spared—for Roosevelt insisted that it be put out of its misery, and one of the other huntsmen obliged with his hunting knife. Also on the President's instructions, the bear was stuffed and sent to the Smithsonian Museum.

It was purely Clifford Berryman's idea to depict the bear as a cub, and on this basis he was surely more precisely the originator of the Teddy Bear—although the President's action, of course, gave him the germ of his idea.

Newspaper reports of the hunting trip—such as those from the *Atlanta (Georgia) Constitution* and the *New York Times*—make no mention whatsoever of a small bear. Indeed, the *Constitution* report specifically headlines its story, 'Roosevelt Refuses to Shoot Old Bear'. It transpires from these accounts that the President was in Mississippi primarily to try and ease the racial tensions between the Whites and the Blacks: the hunting trip in the vicinity of the town of Smedes on the Mississippi delta was purely a diversion. And therefore it is evident that Berryman intended his cartoon to satirise the fact that Roosevelt was proposing to support the small, Black minority in the South. The bear cub was his way of representing the Blacks—and by 'drawing the line in Mississippi' he showed that Roosevelt was a firm believer in Black civil rights.

Berryman's cartoon appeared in the Sunday, November 16 edition of his paper, and it seems likely that Morris Michtom made his toy version within a day or so, although such details are impossible to substantiate. What it *has* been possible to discover is that he produced more than a single bear—and we also know the precise details of these bears.

The version of Berryman's cartoon which Michtom saw had been reprinted in the *New York Times*. It stirred the immigrant's memories of his childhood in Russia where bears were fairly commonplace, and also stimulated his businessman's acumen. Morris was always on the look-out for ideas to attract custom to his stationery and novelty store on Thompson Avenue in Brooklyn. And as he knew that the cartoon had already stimulated a lot of interest, what could be more novel than to make a bear and put it in the window?

Morris mentioned the idea to his wife, Rose. She agreed with him—after all, children were always attracted to stuffed toys, weren't they? And so just like Margarete Steiff across the Atlantic, she sat down and made not one (as legend would have it) but a pair of stuffed bears. To make them look authentic, she chose honey-coloured plush, which she carefully cut into two bear shapes—complete with the familiar 'humped' back—and filled these with excelsior. She used shoe buttons for eyes and noses, and gave them mouths with a line of stitching thread. When finished, the pair stood a grand two-and-a-half feet tall!

The next morning the bears were on display in the window of the Thompson Avenue store—complete with a copy of the cartoon. The selling price was $1.50. Before the day was out—not *immediately* as the story tells us—Morris Michtom had received offers from customers to buy both bears, plus the promise of more orders for any others his wife might make.

(Left) *One of the very earliest American advertisements for teddies—when they were still known as 'Teddy's Bear'.* (Right) *Another rare early teddy advertisement—this one by Morris Michtom's Ideal Novelty Toy Company which eventually became the immensely successful Ideal Toy Corporation.*

The bears were, at this time, still un-named. But an idea for a name was already growing in Morris's head: he would call them 'Teddy's Bears'. Perhaps, though, he should first ask if the President objected to being associated with such toys. A letter was immediately dispatched to the White House asking for permission, before another stitch was sown.

'Dear Mr Michtom,' came the eventual reply, 'I don't think my name is likely to be worth much in the toy bear business, but you are welcome to use it.'

And with that single generous act—imagine if the President had said *No*!—Roosevelt gave the world's most famous soft toy its name, while at the same time giving up a copyright that might well have earned his family untold millions of dollars! On the other hand, he assured himself of an immortality far more spectacular than any which his political life or achievements might have brought him!

The response to the 'Teddy's Bears' among his customers convinced Morris Michtom that he had found a winner. And so, armed with the President's letter, and a sample of the bears, he approached a prominent New York toy wholesaler, Butler Brothers, to seek their wider sales. There, too, the idea was received enthusiastically, and just as model bears had made Margarete Steiff's fortune in Germany, so did they reward Morris in America, launching what has since become one of the largest toy manufacturers in the country, the Ideal Toy Corporation. Within months, people of all ages, all over the country, were clamouring for the bears—and by 1905 there was a craze for Teddy Bears every bit as enthusiastic as the recent vogue for 'Cabbage Patch Dolls'. Indeed, the records of this craze in the Smithsonian Museum show that, whatever Cabbage Patch fans may say, teddies have done it all before!

* * *

Looking through the Museum's files soon reveals how quickly the Teddy Bear had caught the public imagination. President Roosevelt himself very speedily became aware of it, for among the files dealing with his life is a newspaper clipping dated December 1902—less than a month after the incident in Smedes—which is headlined, 'Jokers Send President Teddy's Bear'. Evidently an anonymous person had mailed a small stuffed bear to Roosevelt at the White House, although whether this was intended to embarrass him or not, was never made clear.

What is certain is that Roosevelt capitalised on the public fascination with the Teddy Bear by adopting a bear as his campaign symbol when he campaigned for the Presidency again in 1904 and later in 1912. Manufacturers responded to this by turning out commemorative plates featuring the President and his namesake, as well as stick pins, blazer buttons and scarves. A composer called William R. Haskins wrote what proved to be just one of many songs to feature our little friend, 'Teddy's Bears', and children's games such as 'Feed the Bear' went on sale (similar to that old favourite of pinning a tail on a donkey); there were even jigsaws like 'Teddy and his Bear'.

Clifford K. Berryman watched with a mixture of amazement

and amusement as the furry little toy devised from his cartoon swept the nation. Not for a moment did he regret that he had not copyrighted his idea and thereby enjoyed a flood of royalties.

'I have made thousands of children happy,' he is quoted as saying in one rare interview, 'and that is enough for me.' He did, however, retain the figure of the little bear as a kind of personal trademark, and for years afterwards the 'original' teddy was to be found somewhere or other in all his cartoons! (His skill as a political cartoonist was also recognised in 1944 when he was awarded a Pulitzer Prize.)

It was in 1906 that the 'Teddy Bear Craze' really took a grip of America, as the newspapers and magazines of that period reveal. There are reports in the daily papers of shops all across the country having the utmost difficulty keeping pace with demand, and in the weekly and monthly journals the major stores soon appreciated the value of special advertisements featuring teddies to attract customers. One magazine, called *Playthings*, devoted almost an entire issue to this ever-increasing public interest, under the headline, 'The Plush Bear Craze'. Because it is one of the best contemporary accounts of that amazing time, an extract is included here:

> Never in our history has the country been more at the mercy of bears than it is today. Stuffed plush teddies are fairly rampant, and indications show prospects of a long and continued reign for Majesty Bruin. Department stores are stocking up with them for a while, but not for long, because as soon as the youthful hunters get on their tracks they swoop down and bring them to bay. One New York store, the largest we have, has already sold over sixty thousand teddies, and every week it gets hundreds of dozens which are bought up at once.
>
> The bear rage started at the summer resorts along the Jersey shore, although it originated in New York City. At any rate, a nice, fat, winsome little brown bear sitting on a counter in a boardwalk shop attracted the eyes of a

youngster, and nothing would do but Mamma must stop and look at the lovely plush animal. Mamma liked the bear, too. He was an excellent pocket edition of those big cinnamon bears way up in Bronx Park. The youngster took hold of the coveted plaything and his delight grew. Bruin had such a realistic little hump at the back of his neck, and a voice, too.

The bear's limbs were jointed, and his little pointed head would turn any way you wanted it to, and the soles of his feet—really the bottom of his paws—were all soft and flat and velvety, and he had such dear little ears and black beady eyes. Mamma must buy Bruin for him, the child said. He begged her to, and after a little conversation with the shopkeeper over the price—for the bear was rather an expensive plaything—she finally paid the price and the wistful and anxious eyes of her small son fairly beamed with joy as he marched away hugging his prize just as proudly as a grown-up man or the President of the United States returning from a successful hunt.

That started the bear fad. Of course, every other little boy on the boardwalk had to have a bear. It was just the thing for a boy. Girls had dolls to play with and boys ought to have something like that when it was too hot for baseball or to play Indians. They grew almost eloquent in convincing their mothers of their needs, and soon every shop had sold its stock. So the shopkeepers telegraphed to New York for more and these, too, went like 'hot cakes'. No sooner were the plush figures put in the windows than the shops were swarming with ladies after bears!

By this time, Young America had christened them—and most appropriately, too. Isn't the President the hero of every boy who longs to grow big enough to do the very same things that 'Teddy' Roosevelt does? So Teddy the bear was named, and as Teddy they are now known the length and breadth of our country, as well as on the other side of the Atlantic where they have also appeared.

The *Playthings* report describes precisely the same kind of excitement that greeted the appearance of the Cabbage Patch Dolls. And is not every child's first encounter with a Teddy Bear just as that writer described it, way back in 1906?

And the story doesn't end there—for the Teddy Bear has not confined itself to children. Though it began with youngsters, grown-ups are showing a fondness for these little plush toys, with their attractive bodies and quaint features so full of expression. It did not take long for older people to fall under the enchanting spell of teddies, and now the wonder is: Where *is* it going to end? Habitués of Central Park asked themselves this question the other day when they were confronted by the sight of a pretty young woman dressed in the height of fashion and speeding along in her motor vehicle. By her side was not a girl companion, nor a footman, nor even the accustomed pet bull terrier, but a small Teddy Bear who sat up in solemn state! The girl looked perfectly unconscious that she was doing anything unusual or startling as she rolled past the throngs of pedestrians and threaded her way through the tangle of vehicles moving in a long procession. She instantly became the mark for every eye, and the thought that flashed through the minds of those to whom the sight seemed a novelty

Teddies are all the rage—an advertisement from Playthings *magazine of May 1906.*

was—has Teddy Bear now usurped the place of the pet poodle?

For there he sat, resting one front paw against the side of the vehicle and nestling close to the warm motor coat of his mistress, while his beady eyes gazed straight ahead. From time to time, the girl bent forward to see how he was enjoying the drive, and she gave him an affectionate pat now and then as she spoke to him in a gentle voice. Some thought the bear might have belonged to a small brother or sister, but they were soon convinced of the realness of the fad among older people when, within a quarter of an hour, another automobile whizzed by with a Teddy Bear occupying the seat in the tonneau heretofore held sacred to His Highness the dog.

According to *Playthings*, the fad was also operating across the Atlantic in Great Britain and France, and the magazine again quoted a specific instance from Paris.

Summer visitors in the French capital have become accustomed to seeing beautiful young women carrying Teddy Bears. One lovely mademoiselle was observed in a restaurant with a teddy companion who was given a place by her side, while the erstwhile favourite bat-eared French dog was nursing his feelings all alone outside.

The next thing we suppose we shall be hearing of will be Teddy Bear shows, and then every woman will be trying to buy Blue Ribbon bears with pedigrees as long as your arm. There can surely be no denying the fad is in dead earnest!

An early French advertisement for Teddy Bears. Why the bears should all have their tongues out is a mystery!

As *Playthings* had noted, the 'Teddy Bear Craze' had indeed spread to this side of the Atlantic also, and proof can be found in both the British Library and the British Newspaper Library.

At the beginning of the twentieth century, with Queen Victoria still in power, the maternal instincts of girls were catered for by dolls and dolls' houses, while for boys, toys of anything other than a wholly masculine nature were frowned on. With the coming of the Edwardian era, however, such attitudes changed, and the arrival of the Teddy Bear was as enthusiastically embraced by boys as girls. After all, it was associated with hunting and there were few other animals so strongly masculine in build and temperament. It was also beguiling in expression and soft to the touch—just what girls liked. The other more subtle influences of the bear which we have discussed, were not to become evident until the teddy had proved itself more than just a craze.

Although it is quite evident that Teddy Bears were on sale in Britain within a year or two of their creation, the craze for them as such did not break out until 1912 when, according to one report, over two million teddies were sold during the year! As in America, this demand was accompanied by a host of related items snapped up by adults, including pottery ware, postcards, car mascots, and a variety of fashions from Teddy Bear coats, hats and muffs, to kitchen aprons and even night-dresses!

The magazine *Woman's Home Companion* commented in August 1912, 'The Teddy Bear has been a success with all ages since his very first appearance. All this summer he has been seen at the most fashionable resorts, often displaying a wardrobe fit for a leader of fashion.

'To say that the Teddy Bear has put the nose of the doll out of joint is really to express it mildly. The funny little bear is hugged and loved by more little people in this land than you can count. And as a Christmas present he is showing every sign of being unrivalled . . .'

This view was underlined by another report in *Ladies' Home Journal* which said, 'Teddy is all the rage in the cities. The children carry him to school and even the grown-up ladies carry

The earliest known British advertisement for Teddy Bears—placed by Dean's Rag Book Company in *Home Chat*, November 1908. Very patriotic, too!

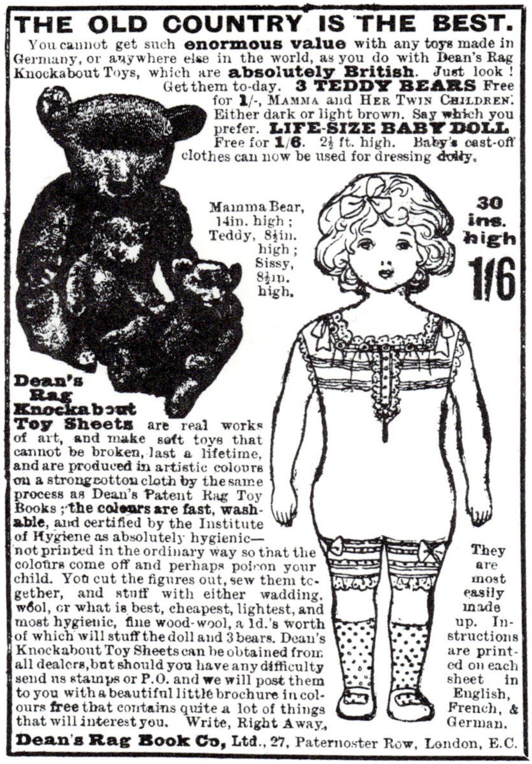

him when they go for a walk, or a ride, or to the theatre.'

The very first manufacturers of Teddy Bears in England were the Dean's Rag Book Company, based in Paternoster Row, London, who began producing their 'absolutely British' teddies in 1908. This versatile company, which had been founded the previous century to produce untearable books for very small children, were never slow to spot a developing trend, and it is no surprise to find them alive and flourishing to this day—still producing an excellent range of teddies.

Dean's were not, however, content with merely copying the American and German bears which were reaching Britain, but instead produced a charming set of three bears, Mamma and her twin cubs, called Teddy and Sissy. A rare old advertisement for this trio of pioneer British teddies is reproduced here.

Another early advertisement, from the following year, offered an equally ingenious variation on the Teddy Bear theme. It was placed in the *Daily Post* of December 14, 1909, by Morrell's Store of Oxford Street in London, and announced for sale: 'Old Mistress Teddy who lived in a shoe.' According to the advertisement, this novelty consisted of one large bear and twelve baby bears, all contained in a large crimson shoe 15 inches long. And the price? Just twenty-one shillings!

This same year also saw the opening in Kingsland, North London, of a shop which specialised in teddies, called 'The Bear Pit'. By far their largest sales were of Steiff bears imported from Germany and, during the last week of September, the shop created a lot of public interest by placing a group of teddies in the window looking suitably solemn and dressed in black. This was to mark the passing of the woman who had jointly begun the whole trend, Margarete Steiff. Already at this time, Steiff bears were being widely regarded as the 'Rolls Royce of Teddy Bears', a distinction they have never lost.

A curious incident in Teddy Bear history is worth mentioning here. In 1912 a certain English manufacturer, J.K. Farnell, claimed to have actually invented the first teddies! This somewhat bold statement was advanced in the firm's advertising, which said that one of their founders, a Miss Farnell, had made a model of a bear in soft fabric as early as 1903. This toy, named 'Alpha Bear', has, however, never been traced, and indeed there are no Farnell bears of any kind still in existence, as far as can be ascertained. Two other early London manufacturers who made rather less sweeping claims for their teddies were W.J. Terry of Dalston, producers of 'Terryer Teddies' and the East London Toy Factory.

Apart from Dean's, two other major British companies have been busy producing teddies for many years, and the older examples of their ranges are now much sought-after by collectors. The first of these is Merrythought Ltd of Ironbridge in Shropshire, whose 'Cheeky Bear' has been a favourite for years; it differs from other teddies in having a very wide grin and being

The much admired Cheeky Bear produced by Merrythought Ltd.

made from simulated mink. Some distinctive bears are also to be found in the range of Chad Valley from Birmingham, with one of the most valuable teddies being 'Englishbear', made in the 'fifties and now a great favourite with American collectors. Also worthy of mention is the Teddy Toy Company which in the early 'thirties was making a Winnie-the-Pooh bear of brown felt with jointed limbs, complete with glass eyes and a delicately sewn nose and mouth. Today examples of this bear are likely to be worth as much as £50 each!

Early in the 1920s, there was a fiendish plot to displace the teddy as the public's favourite soft toy. A group of American manufacturers tried to flood the world's markets with toy possums, but already the Teddy Bear was too well established and the craze for possums soon passed.

An American clergyman with some very strange ideas about teddies went one step further and, in 1907, actually tried to have our furry friends banned! According to this Michigan preacher, 'Race suicide is being fostered, developed and even encouraged by the Teddy Bear! These bundles of horridness are destroying all instincts of motherhood in little girls who now prefer them to their dolls!' Fortunately, teddies everywhere managed to remain immune to this outrageous attack, and their popularity, if anything, increased.

Of course, it was Evelyn Waugh's masterly novel, *Brideshead Revisited*, published in 1945, which gave the English Teddy Bear his slice of literary immortality. For some readers, Aloysius is the real star of the book, and his owner's decline is very much due to his abandonment of his childhood friend with whom he has shared all his intimacies and hopes. Who, after all, deserves our sympathy for leaving behind such a charming, amusing and, above all, talented bear? A bear who, as mentioned earlier, also happened to be based on a real teddy that had belonged to Sir John Betjeman.

How many other famous fictional Teddy Bears were based on real originals? Searching for the answer to this question has brought to light some surprising but intriguing facts which will be revealed in the next chapter . . .

TALES OF THE CELEBEARITIES

Did you know that most of the famous Teddy Bear characters in books and comic strips came into being because their creators were 'bear aware'? If one starts looking into the stories behind such popular fictional heroes as The Roosevelt Bears, Rupert Bear, Teddy Edward, Paddington Bear, Superted and, of course, the best known of them all, Winnie-the-Pooh, sure enough there is a real teddy behind them all. Each and every one of those famous characters owed his inspiration to a furry little friend of the family.

The very first teddy characters were The Roosevelt Bears, created—not surprisingly—in America, but by a man actually born in Canada of Irish immigrant parents. He was Seymour Eaton, and the story of how he created these pioneer teddies (and they were *pioneers* in more ways than one) has been told by his daughter, Mrs Jean Eaton Warren, who lives in New York. Apart from owning copies of some of the very rare books in which, after their initial newspaper appearances, The Roosevelt Bears' adventures were published, she also still has one of Morris Michtom's original teddies which partly inspired the Bears.

Mrs Warren says that her father, Seymour, was very much a wanderer, which probably accounts for the fact that The Roosevelt Bears have most of their adventures travelling around the world. After his birth on a farm in Ontario, Canada, he was sent away from his home to be educated, and as an adult was variously a teacher, the principal of one of the earliest correspondence schools in North America, and then Professor of Business Administration at Drexel College, Philadelphia, where he settled. He also opened the city's first lending library and, after a trip to

Switzerland, had the flash of inspiration which earned him a place in Teddy Bear history as the creator of the first cartoon teddies. For while he was in Switzerland, he bought a pair of model bears for his daughter, Jean.

'It was those that inspired him to create The Roosevelt Bears,' says Mrs Jean Eaton Warren, 'as well as the teddies named after the President, which, of course, gave him the name.

'I've always been very proud of him,' she adds. 'Dad was both creative and promotive. I was only ten when he died suddenly, so I didn't have him for long. He would enter my world of pretend, but best of all were the bedtime stories. I'd pick the subject and he would weave a story about it.'

It was in this very way that Seymour Eaton gave birth to Teddy-B and Teddy-G, two happy-go-lucky bears who had the same restless nature as their creator and were forever getting involved in exciting adventures and narrow escapes. (Their initials, incidentally, stand for their colours, Teddy Brown and Teddy Grey.) In these stories he set a pattern for Teddy Bear stories that has continued to this day.

The tales were first published in a newspaper serial which was illustrated for Eaton by V. Floyd Campbell and later R.K. Culver. Twenty newspapers across the country took up the strip, including the *New York Times*—and to this day 'The Roosevelt Bears' is the only cartoon strip that paper has ever run. The two teddies were an instant success, and soon afterwards were not only republished in book form, but gave rise to such spin-offs as Teddy-B(oy) and Teddy-G(irl) clothes and chinaware bearing their portraits. Children everywhere loved the pair—especially the President's sons in the White House, as Seymour Eaton himself revealed when talking about his phenomenal success in 1907: 'Since the name Roosevelt has been used in the story it may be of public interest to know that President Roosevelt and his boys have been pleased with the story as it appeared in serial form.'

Seymour Eaton's daughter still has in her possession a letter from the Roosevelt family, and recalls that her father numbered

The Roosevelt Bears illustration which prompted the rumour that King Edward VII had been the inspiration for the Teddy Bear.

several other famous men among his acquaintances, including Lord Northcliffe, the English newspaper magnate. Her Dad was, she says, very proud of his British heritage.

Curiously, it is in one of The Roosevelt Bears' adventures that the germ of that story of the Teddy Bear originating in England appears—that it was, in fact, named after King Edward and inspired by that jolly monarch's love of a particular bear cub he saw during a visit to London Zoo. However, in the story 'The Roosevelt Bears Meet King Edward', it is possible to see how the confusion came about. King Edward is himself described as having refused to shoot some 'teddy bears' on his estate because—to use the words Seymour Eaton puts in his mouth, 'It would help me carry my country's cares, if every home had Teddy Bears!'

The author's daughter remembers that after several years of

popularity, The Roosevelt Bears fell into obscurity—only to become the centre of a new wave of interest during World War II.

'It all started because of an article in *Life* magazine,' she says, 'which theorised that Teddy Bears had been inspired by koala bears! I was very indignant about that, and wrote a letter to the magazine which published it, along with a photograph of the Bears. I received well over a hundred letters, and there were many from servicemen who had remembered the books from their childhood. They wanted to know where they could find copies of the books.'

Because the little volumes were already scarce collectors' items, Mrs Warren tried in vain to get them republished, but without the original artwork, publishing techniques at that time were not up to reprinting. It was not until 1980 that she managed to get a small New York reprint publisher to issue a new edition of her father's first book. Her delight at the enthusiastic public reception was matched by the comments of one newspaper critic, Ellen Crean, who wrote, 'Hula-hoops may be out of fashion and skateboards may be going downhill, but here to stay is the Teddy Bear, often the central character in a child's world of fantasy. You may have your Pooh bears, your koala bears, your dancing bears and your 'Bad News Bears', but Teddy Bears started the whole thing off and The Roosevelt Bears book shows how the romance began.'

Mrs Jean Eaton Warren naturally hopes to see more of her father's stories back in print before long, and says happily that the Teddy Bear tradition is continuing as strongly as ever in her family. 'Do you know,' she smiles, 'I've got four grandchildren—and all of them own Teddy Bears. Wouldn't Seymour have been pleased about that?'

* * *

The success of The Roosevelt Bears was not lost on other newspapers, and within a year of their appearance they had competition, both in American and Britain.

As early as the Spring of 1907, the New York magazine *Judge* was running a strip cartoon series called 'Little Johnny and the Teddy Bears' devised and drawn by John Randolph Bray. Although commissioned on the strength of the success of Seymour Eaton's bears, Bray based the high-spirited little boy Johnny on his own son, John jnr, and the teddies who shared his adventures on the six bears his son had already been given by doting relatives.

The serial not only pleased the readers of *Judge*, but also caught the eye of the embryo Hollywood film industry which, even as early as the first decade of this century, was becoming quick to see the potential of transferring cartoon characters to the cinema screen. Bray was signed up to animate 'Little Johnny and the Teddy Bears', devised and drawn by John Randolph Bray. cartoon film. It lasted for just three minutes!

The success of Bray's serial—and Seymour Eaton's great originals—also inspired the Thomas A. Edison Company to make a short feature film in 1908 using real Teddy Bears. The bears appeared to move by way of the 'stop-go' method, where each tiny movement is photographed individually and the film

John Randolph Bray's 'Little Johnny and the Teddy Bears' who were the stars of a cartoon strip, several books and the very first teddy cartoon film, and (right) *the British cartoon strip series, 'Bobby and the Woolly Bears', which was a rather obvious copy.*

LITTLE JOHNNY AND THE TEDDY BEARS

F 1292—Set forth the uproarous adventures of six tuffed Teddy Bears who come to life by means f a wonderful elixer and with Johnny get into and ut of all kinds of mischief. The funniest pictures naginable, by J. R. Bray, reproduuced in brilliant olors and ridiculous rhymes by R. D. Towne, Editor f Judge. Size 14½x10½ inches; bound in stiff card oard, printed in many colors. Each .... **.49**

run through at normal speed, thereby creating the illusion of movement. A rumour that the Edison company used John Bray jnr's teddies in this film has proved impossible to confirm.

In Britain, a boy and his six teddies also made their appearance in a popular weekly magazine, *The Butterfly*, in August 1908. 'Bobby and the Woolly Bears' was a fairly obvious crib from John Bray's original, as can be seen from the two panels from the respective strips illustrated on the previous page. But the series was popular and it did indicate a rapidly growing interest in Teddy Bears on this side of the Atlantic.

When British writers finally came up with Teddy Bear characters of their own, however, the results were, perhaps, the most popular personalities of all.

The year 1920 saw the arrival of Rupert Bear in the pages of the *Daily Express*, beginning a series that has run unbroken to this day. Some people have said that Rupert was created as Britain's answer to Mickey Mouse, but in fact the little bear was a thriving eight-year-old when the rumbustious mouse first appeared on the world's cinema screens. Indeed, although Rupert may not quite be able to match Mickey's phenomenal world-wide success, the adventures of the little bear from Nutwood have been published in 18 countries and the books of stories about him have sold over 100 million copies. After 45 years of non-stop appearance he is Britain's longest running newspaper strip hero. Not bad for a little chap inspired by a small golden teddy bear . . .

Rupert was devised for the *Daily Express* by Mary Tourtel, the artist wife of the newspaper's night editor, Herbert Tourtel. The challenge to provide a popular character for the paper's young readers was one that Mary could not resist—for challenges were things she had never been afraid of. Born in Canterbury in 1874, she was the daughter of a stained-glass expert who spent many years working on the town's magnificent cathedral. She became interested in drawing while very young, no doubt inspired by her eldest brother, Ernest, who became a first-class artist and illustrated the famous work *Jock of the Bushveld*. Mary went to Canterbury College of Art and there won a gold medal as the

One of Mary Tourtel's original drawings of Rupert, and (left) a rare portrait of Mary herself.

outstanding pupil of her year. Her work then was said to have shown the influence of Beatrix Potter.

Mary was not just a serious art student, however. She loved adventure, and in 1919, after her marriage to Herbert Tourtel, she flew a Handley-Page aeroplane from Hounslow to Brussels in a record time. On board during this trip was a small, golden-brown Teddy Bear she had been given for luck. After that, the little mascot was never far from her side, and she used him for a model when she began the Rupert series for the *Express*.

Mary had, in fact, already illustrated several children's books featuring animal characters, and her skill at portraying animals was enhanced by her habit of taking a sketch book with her whenever she was out walking in the country, so that she could make drawings of birds and animals in the wild.

Within a short time, Rupert and his pals Bill Badger, Algy Pug, Edward Trunk, Podgy Pig and the others had become famous throughout the land—and boosted the circulation of the *Daily Express* into the bargain. Years later, the paper's owner, Lord Beaverbrook, was to say that Rupert 'did more for the rise in sales than the famous Crusader symbol'. There were soon spin-offs galore: the Rupert League, annuals, crayoning books, jigsaw puzzles and all kinds of merchandising on which the bear's happy little figure appeared. It was enough to bring an even bigger smile to the face of Mary Tourtel's little teddy in her studio, let alone Lord Beaverbrook and the Editor of the *Express*! Despite this success, however, Rupert did not change in character or appearance, and indeed his jersey, scarf and checked trousers (six bands precisely) have remained constant to this day.

Mary Tourtel herself continued to draw Rupert until 1935 when failing eyesight caused her to give up the job. At this point the task was taken up by another skilled illustrator, Alfred Bestell, who drew the strip unbroken for 30 years, and although he contributed immeasurably to the continuing success of the strip, has sometimes mistakenly been credited as the originator. Despite her success at creating a legend who has delighted generations of readers, Mary's own later life was dogged with misfortune. She was unable to have children, and apart from her declining eyesight, also had to nurse her husband through a serious illness which led to his death in 1931. She lived on comfortably, thanks to a golden handshake from the *Daily Express*, and died in a Canterbury hotel in 1948, the golden teddy bear, now somewhat shabby, still on her mantelpiece.

Over the years since Rupert's first appearance, there has been a good deal of speculation as to why this little chap, with his unmistakable Teddy Bear head yet human body, should have proved so popular when other strip contemporaries like Teddy Tail have fallen by the wayside. We think the historian of children's literature, Mary Cadogan, was closest to the answer when she wrote on the 60th Anniversary of his birth in 1980:

> It is interesting to speculate why he has outlived his competitors. Many of them emanate as much exuberance and charm as Rupert, and they give the reader the same feeling of well-being. But—with the possible exception of Pooh Bear—the stories in which they are featured lack Rupert's magical, timeless element. And Rupert is possibly more humanised. Parents as well as children appreciate him—and not only nostalgically; he is in a sense an ideal son—considerate, bright, well-mannered; able to go through fire and water without getting his immaculate red jersey and checked trousers torn or dirty.

These views are also shared by two of Rupert's most famous fans—and teddy owners, to boot—Paul McCartney and Lord Montagu of Beaulieu. Singer McCartney has recently made a delightful animated short film called *Rupert and the Frog Song*. And when Lord Montagu was asked what was his happiest childhood memory, he replied, 'When we were very small, the daily papers were delivered to the nursery and we were encouraged to look at them and, later, to read them. It was then that I fell in love with Rupert the Bear in the *Daily Express* cartoon strip. I couldn't wait to open the paper to see what Rupert was up to—real rip-roaring adventures!'

Rupert was just six years old when his even more famous rival, Winnie-the-Pooh, appeared. The story of his genesis is one of the most fascinating in Teddy Bearology.

The man behind this creation was, of course, A.A. Milne, a playwright and regular contributor to the magazine *Punch*. Although it was to be an actual Teddy Bear that prompted Pooh's birth, the influence of 'bear awareness' came into Milne's life when he was still a fifteen-year-old scholar at Westminster School in London. John Rae, who is the headmaster of that distinguished seat of learning, explains what happened.

> It was customary for the Epilogue of the annual Latin play performed by the scholars of Westminster School to comment on current events. In 1897 the gold rush to the Yukon provided a target. A gentleman who had gone to the Klondyke entered and was greeted as a polar bear, '*Quis hic nunc advenit ursa polaris*?' The gold rush polar bear was played by F.T. Barrington-Ward . . . and in the audience each night or helping behind the scenes was another scholar, A.A. Milne, whose own distinctive version of the polar bear later struck it rich on a scale that most gold prospectors could only experience in their dreams.

That was part one of the creation of Pooh. Part two occurred nearly a quarter of a century later when A.A. Milne was 38 years old, married to a beautiful young girl named Daphne, ten years younger than himself, and the father of a one-year-old son, Christopher Robin. For the child's first birthday, Mrs Milne went to the famous London store, Harrods, and there bought a chubby, golden-brown Teddy Bear, which she took to the family home in Chelsea. In the years that followed, the teddy became a firm favourite with Christopher Robin who, as soon as he could talk, began to ask his father to tell him stories about the bear. How the little creature got his name has also puzzled generations of readers, although the mystery has now been explained by Laurence Irving, a life-long friend of the family.

Mr Irving, a theatrical designer and costumier, had become

A. A. Milne, his son Christopher Robin and the teddy that made them immortal, from the portrait by Howard Cocter.

friendly with A.A. Milne when they worked together on some stage reviews, for which Milne had contributed sketches. It was during the run of one particularly successful revue, *Vaudeville Vanities*, that the fateful event occurred.

Among those who had contributed sketches and lyrics for the production were John Hastings Turner and Alan Milne.

> Their children, Anne and 'Billy' (Christopher Robin), were about the same age as my daughter, Pamela. During the long run of the revue, to celebrate Pamela's fifth birthday, my wife and I invited Anne, Billy and their mamas to join us in a visit to the London Zoo prior to a tea party in our home at Cumberland Terrace.
>
> Our favourite inmate was a brown bear that had her den in the bowels of the Mappin Terraces where she would receive us and our proffered tit-bits with engaging courtesy. She had been the mascot of a Canadian regiment and had been left in the care of the Zoological Society. Her name was Winnie.
>
> I had planned with a friendly keeper that the final *coup de théâtre* if our expedition would be the presentation of the children to Winnie in her lair. In due course they followed our guide into the dark cavern leading to the iron grille of Winnie's cage. When he opened it, Winnie—as was her custom—ambled out to greet her visitors. No doubt, in the narrow confines of the tunnel, to the children she appeared monstrous. The girls held their ground. Billy wavered, retreated a step or two, then overcame his awe and joined the girls in feeding and making much of the docile bear. Our guests declared that it had been a wonderful surprise.
>
> The first hint I received of its historical consequences was from John Hastings Turner. With mischievous glee he described to me how at another party Billy's mother, Daphne, had recounted that confrontation and its endearing climax when her Billy had embraced Winnie as he sighed ecstatically, 'Oh, Pooh!'

The teddy which Mrs Milne had bought at Harrods had been rather prosaically named Edward, and the re-naming, Winnie-the-Pooh, came about when the bear became the star of A.A. Milne's stories. The stories of Christopher Robin and his adventures with Pooh were shaped for publication by Milne retelling them to his wife who took them down in long-hand. On the fiftieth anniversary of Pooh's birth, Mrs Milne was to recall those days:

> My husband dictated the stories to me. I didn't type or anything, but he needed an audience to react. He would walk to and fro puffing at his pipe while I wrote and laughed . . . We had fun in a world of special intimacy and utter silliness, laughing at ridiculous jokes and talking in our own special language. We were all acting little incidents with Pooh and the nursery animals the whole time—we were all quite idiotic about it. Looking back to those days I always see Pooh and the small boy with whom we shared them . . . with his large brown eyes and beautiful corn-coloured hair cut square.

As many readers may be aware, Christopher Robin Milne has rarely talked about his central role in the creation of this phenomenon, but in 1974 he was induced to reveal some details of his relationship with Pooh.

'He was the oldest of my toys,' he said, 'only a year younger than I was, and my inseparable companion. As you find us in the poem "Us Two", so we were in real life. Every child has his favourite toy, and every only-child has a special need for one. Pooh was mine, and probably, clasped in my arms, not very different from the countless other bears clasped in the arms of countless other children. From time to time he went to the cleaners, and from time to time ears had to be sewn on again, lost eyes replaced and paws renewed.'

And of the actual creation of the stories by his father, Christopher Milne added, 'It started in the nursery; it started with me. And as I played with the toys and talked to them and gave them voices to answer with, so they began to breathe. But alone I couldn't take them very far. I needed help. So my mother joined me and she and I and the toys played together, and gradually more life, more character flowed into them, until they reached a point at which my father could take over. The Pooh in my arms, the Pooh sitting opposite me at the breakfast table, was a Pooh who had climbed trees in search of honey, who had got stuck in a rabbit hole, who was a "bear with no brain at all".'

One must not forget, of course, that part of the success of Pooh was also due to the choice of Ernest Shepard as his illustrator—a fact which A.A. Milne initially deplored. 'What on earth do you see in that man?' he is said to have enquired of his publisher on looking at some samples. 'He is perfectly hopeless.'

Later Milne was happy to admit he was quite wrong, for the combination of these two men was as critical in its way as that of Lewis Carroll and John Tenniel in creating the enduring images of *Alice in Wonderland*.

It is not generally known, however, that Ernest Shepard did *not* base his drawings for Pooh on Christopher Milne's teddy, but on a bear belonging to his own son, Graham, a rather magnificent creature called Growler. This much-loved bear sadly never achieved the fame to which he was entitled, and met a rather sorry end when he was passed on to Graham Shephard's own daughter, Minette, and was 'worried to death' by a dog while living in war-time exile in Canada.

The Pooh books still continue to sell by the million, and the little bear has become the star of innumerable items of merchandise, as well as one of Walt Disney's most colourful full-length cartoon films. He also has the distinction of being the only teddy to have a street named after him—'Ulica Kubusia Puchatka' in Warsaw, Poland, complete with the familiar Shepard outline—while a 23-year-old model of him became the world champion parachuting teddy when he dropped 3,800 feet in a three-foot parachute over Florida!

Walt Disney's Pooh makes a joke at the expense of another member of the Roosevelt family.

Today, the original Pooh sits in a brightly lit place of honour in the reception room of his American publishers, E.P. Dutton. He is regularly visited by admirers of all ages from all over the world. Very occasionally he returns to Britain for some special function and—being fiercely patriotic—insists on flying British Airways (first class, of course, as is only right and proper for surely the most famous Teddy Bear of all).

* * *

Another character who has become an international favourite, also inspired by a teddy bought in a famous London store, is Paddington Bear. In 1983 Selfridge's featured Paddington's Grotto as its Christmas attraction. To many people it may have seemed strange that the marmalade-loving bear from Peru, in his duffle coat and wellington boots, should replace Father Christmas, but those in the know were aware that it was in this very store, 25 years earlier, that Paddington's creator, Michael Bond, had found the Teddy Bear which has made him a household name.

'It was Christmas Eve, 1956, and I was trying to do some last-minute shopping,' Michael told us. 'I wandered into Selfridge's and there, on this shelf for glassware, I saw this Teddy Bear. He looked so fed-up! In fact he seemed so lonely that I couldn't bear the thought of him spending Christmas there and so I bought him as a present for my wife.'

At that moment Michael, who had worked in a solicitor's office before the war and then become a BBC TV cameraman, had no other thoughts about the bear than that he would make a nice present. But that act of kindness, by a man who had never considered himself 'bear aware', was to be rewarded by fame and fortune beyond his wildest dreams.

Over the next few weeks, the sight of the little brown Teddy Bear on his wife's dressing-table kept putting ideas into his head. Finally, Michael decided to weave a story around him. As he was living near Paddington station, he had no trouble with a name for the character. Having given him a Peruvian background, he dumped him on the platform of the London station where he was found by the Brown family with whom he thereafter shared his life and adventures. Michael wrote more for his own amusement than with any thoughts of publication and, ten days later, *A Bear Called Paddington* was complete. He was not overly optimistic when his wife pressed him to submit the story, and indeed there are a number of London publishing houses that still blush with shame at having turned down what was to prove the first of an immensely successful series. Michael, however, took the success very matter-of-factly.

'I've never considered myself a serious writer,' he reminisces today, 'but I am interested in characters who aren't masters of their destiny. Put into situations, as Paddington is, they create events.'

The events that Paddington created outside the books were extraordinary, too. In the space of a few years the stories were being translated into 20 different languages, including Russian and Greek, a television series was made and all manner of merchandising, from stickers to birthday mugs, was launched. A Paddington teddy was also enthusiastically received by young fans—but why the boots, some asked, as he had none in the book illustrations by Peggy Fortnum?

'He's a bear for standing up in the corner,' smiles Michael Bond. 'That's why he wears wellington boots!'

He also admits that a number of Paddington's escapades are based on his own experiences. For instance, he did once actually wallpaper over a door, as happens in *More about Paddington*, and he also got into considerable trouble the first time he tried to make some dumplings! Michael confesses to loving marmalade and duffle coats, too!

'Paddington's strength is that he's like the small man up against life's problems,' he says. 'He operates in contemporary life—like dealing with launderettes. But then he goes back to an almost pre-war home—ordered and safe.'

Michael Bond and the bear who made him famous, Paddington.

To date, over 350 Paddington products have been licensed around the world. One of the places where he is most popular is Japan, where a number of 'Paddington Stations' have been opened which sell nothing but items relating to the little chap! To mark his 25th anniversary in 1983, a television special was made which featured Paddington dancing to the sound track of 'Singin' in the Rain'.

Paddington has certainly come a long way from that shelf in Selfridge's, and no doubt there are many more marmalade years before him. He will, however, remain immortally young, and continue to celebrate two birthdays—'Just like the Queen,' as Mrs Bird observes in one of the stories, 'so you ought to consider yourself very important.' But just imagine if Michael Bond had *not* picked up that lonely little bear in the store . . .

* * *

While all the famous teddies mentioned so far have appealed to adults as well as children, Teddy Edward, who came on the scene in 1962, is very much a young children's favourite. He was created by Patrick and Mollie Matthews and, once again, was a teddy that had belonged to the couple's daughter, Sarah, who was two years old when the saga began.

Patrick Matthews says that a photograph he had taken of a cat belonging to Cecil Beaton was also part of the Teddy Edward story. Patrick, who worked for *Vogue* magazine, had photographed the cat sitting in a flower bed, and a framed enlargement of this picture hung in their daughter's bedroom. One day, Mollie suggested that it might be a good idea to take photographs of soft toys that could be framed in the same way for hanging in nurseries. Better still, she said, why not do a book of such photographs featuring Sarah's favourite, Teddy Edward, and his friends?

The idea was a winner, and five Teddy Edward books appeared in the early 1960s, selling over a quarter of a million copies. Enid Blyton was among those who praised the books, commenting,

'Teddy Edward seems to do all the things that every child would want his or her own Teddy Bears to do.'

Fame also brought problems for Teddy Edward; apart from being a photographic model, he was also Sarah's constant companion, and like all much-loved teddies he began to show signs of wear. The result was that a new bear had to be found—and this proved no easy matter.

When it became increasingly obvious that Patrick and Mollie would never find a perfectly matched substitute, a visit to a doll's hospital for Teddy Edward and Teddy Edward II was called for. There the new bear had his face 'lifted' so that no one could tell the difference between the two. After this ordeal, the original Teddy Edward was allowed to go into cosy retirement in Sarah's room.

Although, as early as 1965, the Matthews had considered putting Teddy Edward on television, pressure of work prevented this happening until 1971. Then a series of 13 stories was made which took the delightful little bear to such exotic places as Greece, Spain, France, Switzerland, as well as the West Coast of Ireland and around the Matthews' own little water bailiff's cottage—all of which offered many ideal locations for photography.

Since then books and TV films have continued, taking Teddy Edward to audiences all over the world—just as the Matthews themselves have been busy taking the little bear to new and still more exciting places as the backdrop to his adventures. He has journeyed down the River Niger in a pirogue, visited Timbuctoo to see the Dogon dancers, and in the Sahara Desert met up with the colourful tribes of Tuaregs, Bozos and Peuhls. He has visited Everest, too, being flown in an Air India jet as a 'VIB' (Very Important Bear) and has well-earned his title of a 'Much Travelled Bear'.

Patrick Matthews particularly remembers the two young waitresses who approached him in a Swiss hotel and asked him if he was photographing Teddy Edward at the time. Somewhat taken aback, he asked why they wanted to know. Oh, they

Teddy Edward—the only Teddy Bear to appear as himself in photographic stories.

explained, they were New Zealanders working their way around the world, and they had been brought up on Teddy Edward's travel books when they were young!

Although the stories of Teddy Edward are for young children, the little teddy's adventures so caught the interest of *Harper's* magazine, that he has had to write special reports for their travel issues on the Sahara visit and the trip to Mount Everest! We wish them all happy travelling in the future.

* * *

And so we come to the latest teddy tale of success—the up-to-the-minute SuperTed who seems to typify the present worldwide outburst of enthusiasm for teddies and all things Teddy Bearish. In the stories of SuperTed, his creator, Mike Young, has taken the traditional qualities of the Teddy Bear and mingled them with the attributes of a super-hero, which is what a good many children now want of their characters.

SuperTed is already an established international success, the books about him having been translated into 13 languages and his televised adventures being shown in 35 countries. In the best tradition of all our success stories, the little teddy with the super powers was created in the most ordinary manner—in fact, he owes his birth to a little boy who was afraid of the dark.

The story begins one evening in 1978, in the small town of Pentyrch outside Cardiff, when Mike Young was trying to get his four-year-old son, Richard, off to sleep.

'The trouble was he was afraid of the dark,' Mike remembers, 'and I was forever trying to think up stories to take his mind off it. And then suddenly I got this bit of inspiration from the Teddy Bear Richard was clutching. I had the idea of a Teddy Bear who was also afraid of the dark, but who could say magic words, peel off his fur, reveal a flying suit and cape, and go off on all sorts of adventures to help people and animals. Richard loved it, and I had to keep making up stories about SuperTed, as I called him.'

Sensing that other children might like the Teddy Bear as much as his son, Mike decided to give up his job manufacturing artificial flower displays and see if he could make a living from SuperTed. 'It was a terrible gamble,' he says, 'but somehow SuperTed took over, and I sank all my savings into forming a company and publishing the first SuperTed books.'

Anyone with any experience in publishing will quickly tell you the odds against such a gamble. For to publish a book is one thing, to get it into the shops and then have people buy it can be quite another matter. And indeed, Mike is quick to admit that his idea did not get off to a very promising start. Sales of those early SuperTed titles were decidedly slow.

But then fate intervened in the shape of Chris Grace, the head of marketing and planning at *Sianel Pedwar Cymru*, the Welsh fourth television channel which broadcasts most of its programmes in Welsh at peak viewing hours. He was looking for a

The latest teddy hero—Mike Young's SuperTed, soon to be a Walt Disney star, too.

new children's series, and thought that Mike's character might just work on television.

So SuperTed made his debut—in Welsh, mind you—in November 1982. He was an immediate hit, and the following year was transmitted in English, too. The TV success, not surprisingly, gave a boost to the SuperTed books and, in no time at all, the little teddy's catchwords, such as 'galloping grapefruits' and 'rocketing raspberries', could be heard in streets and playgrounds everywhere. It was a double triumph for Mike—SuperTed had not only cured his son Richard of his fear of the dark, but was well on the way to making him a rich man!

The real accolade for the series came when the Walt Disney organisation decided to buy SuperTed for America—the first British cartoon series ever bought by that revered company. The news was greeted by one enthusiastic English journalist in these words: 'Galloping grapefruits! Watch out, Mickey Mouse. Here comes SuperTed, the little Teddy Bear from Wales who is taking the United States by storm. SuperTed has flown into the big league and big dollars—this crime-fighting bear could become a multi-million dollar industry in America!'

Like the other famous teddies of fiction, SuperTed is now being merchandised on jogging suits, caps, T-shirts, pyjamas, bags, and an ever increasing number of books as Mike Young continues to write new stories. Yet why does he think the little bear proved so attractive to the Walt Disney organisation, with all their facilities for creating material themselves?

'They liked him because he was a soft, non-violent little character, a bit vulnerable,' Mike says. He adds that initially the Disney people had planned to give the SuperTed characters American accents, but when the series was shown to some children in Los Angeles, they particularly liked the English accents provided by the former star of *Doctor Who*, Jon Pertwee, and those two fine comic character actors, Melvyn Hayes and Roy Kinnear. So the soundtrack will remain unchanged.

So now a British teddy is taking the very home of Teddy Bears by storm. Will our furry friends ever cease to surprise us?

BEAR HAPPENINGS

There are hundreds of examples, from all over the world, of the power of Teddy Bears to aid the recovery of hospital patients of all ages. Those described below are typical of many stories of bears that 'heal'.

Ten-year-old Tony McDermott, of Erith in Kent, underwent a kidney transplant in 1979. He had a total of twelve operations and was sustained through them all by the constant companionship of his teddy, Bobby McDermott. This remarkable partnership came to light when Tony won a contest run by the *Sunday Mirror* which invited young readers to write about 'Me and My Teddy Bear'. Tony's heart-warming words won the unanimous approval of the judges:

'My Teddy is called Bobby McDermott', he wrote, 'and he has been with me for twelve operations and always comes into hospital with me. He comforts me.'

After being declared the winner while he was still in Guy's Hospital, London, Tony explained about his bear. 'He was given to me by an aunt when I was born,' he said. 'It's as if he has kept following me ever since. I first went into hospital when I was five and a year later I was living on a kidney machine.'

It was not until he was ten that Tony could have the kidney transplant, and even then a set-back meant he had to stay in plaster from the waist down for over a month. But all the time there was Bobby to cheer him up.

'Bobby also needed an operation,' he said. 'He had some stuffing trickling down his neck, so the surgeon bandaged him up after he'd finished with me.

Tony's prize was a trip to Vienna, and a highlight of the stay was a specially arranged Teddy Bears' Picnic in the famous Vienna woods, at which Bobby was the guest of honour. 'It was very nice,' Tony said on his return, 'and I enjoyed meeting all those other bears. But even if I saw a million other teddies I'd still rather have Bobby!' (The *Sunday Mirror*, incidentally, is obviously well aware of Teddy Bear appeal and runs a regular column about a 9 foot 4 inches high bear called Big Ted—made by Chad Valley—who travels about the country meeting young readers.)

Mrs Joanne Blume of New York, who spent many years in considerable pain before undergoing the necessary operation to relieve her suffering, says that she got the strength for this when she rediscovered her old childhood teddy.

'Eddie had been given to me when I was small,' she recalls, 'and I have to confess that when I left home I forgot all about him and left him behind. I didn't have much luck in my life for several years—I lost one job after another and then I made a bad marriage. To top it all I developed a serious abdominal condition. Somehow after all my bad luck I just couldn't bring myself to go to hospital.

'Then, during a visit to my parents' home, I found Eddie at the back of a cupboard. His face looked reproachful, but somehow glad to see me. I'm not ashamed to say it brought a lump to my throat and a tear to my eye. I think I just sat on the bed and cuddled the little chap for hours. As I did so, I suddenly began to feel better for the first time in years. I later realised it must be a sign—and I decided to have the operation. With Eddie by my side, I reckoned I could face it now.'

While Mrs Blume was in hospital, a sympathetic nurse who understood her fear of the operation—and who must have been a Teddy Bear lover, too—prepared Eddie for the operation just like his mistress. And when Joanne recovered afterwards, she found a red scar mark on the bear's stomach exactly the same as her own!

'As you can imagine,' Mrs Blume says, 'I wouldn't be parted from my bear for the world now. And I wonder sometimes

Teddy can be a great source of comfort to patients, young and old, in hospital. This bear, one of Steiff's most appealing modern teddies, would be a perfect hospital companion.

whether things might have been different if I had not left Eddie behind when I left home.'

Another person whose fortunes were changed by a Teddy Bear was Malcolm Wilson of Ontario in Canada. He had never actually owned a teddy as a child, and when he went into hospital for an operation was overcome by a terrible sense of foreboding.

'I just got it into my head that I was going to die,' he recalls. 'Not long before the operation, this lovely old lady in one of the adjacent wards, who used to go visiting other patients who were confined to bed, stopped to talk to me. She was carrying this battered old Teddy Bear under her arm.

'She had a lovely soothing voice, and she told me that the bear had been her friend all her life and gave her great strength whenever she was upset or ill. She said that whenever she found patients who were worried about their operations she offered to lend them the bear. Now my first thought was that perhaps she was a bit dotty. Me be seen with a Teddy Bear, I thought, at my age! But she was so reassuring, that in the end I hadn't the heart to refuse her. I was still a bit embarrassed, though.

'Well,' Malcolm continues, 'I came out of that operation feeling marvellous—and there, still clutched in my hand, was the paw of the Teddy Bear. One of the nurses said I had never let go of it throughout the entire operation! When the lady came back for her treasured little possession, I had to admit that he had been a great help. And when I left hospital I immediately bought a teddy of my own—now I've got 35 of them in the happiest little den you've ever seen!'

* * *

People of all ages have reason to be grateful to their teddies. Take the case of little orphan Alison Matthews, now nearly ten, who loves cuddling her bears—and is only alive today because of a miracle brought about by one of them in May 1977. She was then just eighteen months old and in a car being driven by her 21-year-old father, David Matthews, and her mother, Petula, travelling home to Birkenhead in Cheshire. Alison was strapped in a safety-seat in the back of the car.

On the M53 motorway through the Wirral, the car went out of control. It struck an eight-inch wide direction sign and was sliced in two. The wreckage tumbled twenty feet down an embankment, completely out of sight of the road.

Alison's Teddy Bear, which had been in her arms, was among the items from the car which were strewn along the embankment slope, but nothing could be seen by passing motorists. Ten minutes after the crash a police patrol car actually passed the spot—but carried on.

It was some time later, in fact, and for no reason he can quite explain, that Cyril Washington, a car plant worker, pulled his motorbike over to the hard shoulder, stopped and looked down. Immediately spotting the wreckage of the car, he went to investigate, and found the young father crushed to death. Mrs Matthews he discovered seventy yards away, having evidently died while trying to crawl for help.

Horrified by what he could see, Mr Washington was just about to go and call the police, when he noticed the Teddy Bear lying spread-eagled and very plaintive-looking on the ground. Could there have been a child in the crash, he wondered? Cautiously, he peered into the severed rear section of the wreck. And there, dangling upside down in her safety straps, was baby Alison. Her lonely ordeal had lasted all of three hours.

'I felt she must be dead,' recalls Mr Washington. 'But I released her, and took her gently into my arms to lay her down. All of a sudden her eyelids flickered and I realised she was alive. I wrapped her in my coat, carried her up the embankment, and rang the police who rushed her to hospital.'

In fact Alison had a hairline fracture, a black eye and was suffering from shock. It was definitely touch-and-go for her life as she lay on the critical list for 48 hours. But she recovered and today lives with her grandparents, a living testimony to the silent appeal of a Teddy Bear.

A perhaps even more miraculous escape occurred in Spain in April 1985, when a teddy saved a two-year-old girl from being crushed to death by a falling body!

The accident happened in a small street in Palma, Majorca, on a sun-filled morning. Little Maria Gomes was playing in the street with a large-size teddy she had been given as a birthday present just the day before.

Suddenly, as she cuddled the bear happily, a woman plunged from a sixth floor balcony directly overhead. Quite unaware of the danger, Maria would certainly have been killed had not the bear cushioned the impact, and she could also have been crushed by the woman's body but for the teddy's soft protection.

Rescuers who pulled the little girl and her teddy from under the dead woman, found them both unhurt. It was an escape almost beyond belief, they and the child's parents agreed.

Yet another remarkable story comes from Australia, where a Teddy Bear lover and her family were saved from a fire in their home by a teddy.

Mrs Edith Thomson, who lives in Melbourne with her husband and two teenage sons, was asleep in her home in August 1981 when, unbeknown to her, a fire broke out in the lounge below.

'I was absolutely sound asleep when I gradually became conscious of this growling noise,' she says. 'At first I took no notice, but every time I moved in bed it seemed to get louder. Finally, I sat up in bed and at once thought I could smell something. When I turned on the bedside light, there was smoke beginning to curl under the bedroom door and I could hear the crackle of flames.

'I immediately woke my husband and told him what was happening. He rushed to the door and could see that the house was on fire down below. We both went through an adjoining door and wakened our boys. Fortunately we have a sloping roof just

The bionic 'Snoozy Bear' which helps soothe crying babies, designed by Andrew Page in 1980.

below our bedroom window, so we were all able to scramble out and slide to safety.'

It was only when the fire brigade were busy putting out the blaze that Mrs Thomson remembered the growling sound that had woken her up.

'I couldn't think for a while what it might have been,' she says. 'And then suddenly I remembered my faithful old Teddy Bear, Toby, which I've had since a child and which often sleeps with me. The growling sound I had heard had been just like the one he made when he was squeezed. But I hadn't been squeezing him in my sleep. Could he have warned me? I thought it most likely I had probably rolled over him and that had caused the noises which woke me up. But whichever was the case, I knew that my family and I probably owed our lives to him!'

Luckily, too, the firemen managed to halt the blaze in the Thomson home before it destroyed the bedrooms, and Toby was found unharmed. Since that day, says Mrs Thomson, his growl has always had a kind of smoky quality about it!

One other accident story has an amusing slant to it, and happily the outcome was not fatal.

It concerns Mr Osborne Clarke of Swindon who, one bright summer's day a few years ago, was having a picnic in a bluebell wood near his home. Selecting a picturesque spot among the carpet of pretty flowers, he and his companions sat quietly enjoying themselves, until a car went by.

The motorist took one look at the scene, let his mouth drop open, and then promptly swerved the car off the road into the ditch.

Mr Clarke, a keen amateur photographer, still wonders why the driver's reaction should have been so violent—after all, he and his 25 Teddy Bears had only been enjoying the warm weather and picnicking!

Mr Clarke has one favourite bear, Podge, who often accompanies him and his wife when they go on camping holidays.

'He has his own sleeping bag made out of a balaclava hat,' says

Mr. Clarke. 'Our friends are usually quite unaffected by it, although I suppose they must have wondered what was happening when we recorded the tune of "Teddy Bears' Picnic" on the organ of a church we visited!'

* * *

Here are three more stories that simply couldn't be left out. The first is from a Mrs Smith of London in a letter to the *Sunday People*.

'On my only daughter's second birthday,' she wrote, 'she was given a large doll and a big brown Teddy Bear. Thirty years later they are still in her old room.

'Her two little girls often play with them and on their last visit the eldest wanted to take the Teddy Bear home.

'"No," said my daughter. "She can't do that—it's mine!"'

The second, from John Mullis, of Shaftesbury in Dorset, is a little gem.

'My friend's little girl has given the name Gladly to her beloved Teddy Bear,' he wrote to the *Sunday Mirror*, 'which happens to be cross-eyed. Asked to explain the name, she said, "We sing about my teddy in church. It's a hymn called 'Gladly my cross-eyed bear'."'

The third again comes from the *Sunday People*. It was a letter from Mrs I. Evans of Corwen in Clwyd who wrote:

'A neighbour's little boy was allowed to use some of his old baby clothes to dress his Teddy Bear. When a new baby arrived, however, the clothes were needed again and teddy lost his wardrobe.

'Visitors who admired the new baby were very quickly informed by big brother—"He's got Mum's eyes, Daddy's mouth, and my teddy's clothes!"'

* * *

There are innumerable tales about Teddy Bear growlers; here are three of the best of them.

The unlikely bear that says, 'Woof! Woof!'

The first is illustrated by the little sketch taken from an American magazine, offering as a free gift a teddy who says 'Woof! Woof!'

The second concerns a friend whose faithful old bear lost his voice one day after a lifetime of service. The lady in question decided on giving Ted a new growler and promptly despatched him for some attention.

Imagine her horror when the fellow was returned not with a splendid growl, but a most plaintive moo! The restorer apologised that he had run out of growls!

The experience of Mrs Doreen Jones of Hanham near Bristol was one that has perhaps been shared by other readers.

For when her six-year-old daughter walked through the security check at Heathrow, the alarm suddenly went off. And it proved to be the metal growler in the teddy under the child's arm which had set it off!

* * *

Teddy Bears have done some unusual jobs in their time—but none stranger than acting as foster mother to a baby monkey!

This happened in October 1979 when a baby Spider Monkey at Blackpool Zoo was rejected by his mother because he was 'too clinging', according to his keeper.

Worried about the little monkey's survival, the keeper—who knew something about teddies and the fact that they could take any amount of cuddling—decided to introduce him to a bear. The two immediately became bosom pals, and Pedro the monkey has refused to be parted from his 'mother-figure' ever since.

* * *

The Teddy Bear lover with one of the nicest jobs of all is John Darcy Noble, the toy curator of the Museum of the City of New York. He has a collection of 15 superb teddies in the museum—as well as a hug of his own at home. Despite this, he still remains inconsolable over the loss of his childhood teddy.

'I was born on your side of the Atlantic,' he said. 'And during the Second World War I served as a fire-fighter. I always carried this little teddy in my pocket, and then during the London Blitz he went missing. I don't know if he was burned in the flames or crushed by rubble, but it was the worst thing that happened to me in the war.'

All the bears in the museum have their own stories to tell, says John, but his favourite is the distinguished teddy which had been sent to him by a nun. 'She had been allowed to keep him when she took her vows,' he explained, 'but she was not allowed to pass him on to another nun 45 years later. So he came to join us, and in deference to his previous life I try to allow him as much seclusion as I can!'

John also tells two other interesting stories which in their different ways illustrate the hold that the Teddy Bear has now got on America.

The first concerns a young woman who was walking through a well-known department store. Reaching the second floor, she stopped to gaze in wonderment at the row upon row of Teddy Bears that faced her. There were teddies stacked on shelves, teddies piled on counters, teddies hanging from Christmas trees. (For it was Christmas time, you see.)

There were teddies in Santa Claus suits, in sweaters, in dresses and in duffle coats. There were bears small enough to fit into pockets and bears large enough to be home furnishings. As if in a dream, the woman picked up one bear after another, until at last she found one that she couldn't put down.

'I came looking for a bear for a little child,' she finally told an assistant who came over to see if she could help, 'but I may have to buy him for myself.'

In contrast to this rather touching story, John Noble says that because of the tremendous interest in Teddy Bears, some rather unfeeling people are now actually using them to indicate their sexual proclivities. Without wishing to offend the sensibilities of any furry friends who might be reading this book, it seems that bears are now being carried in the back pockets of jeans with their paws tied together, in leather straps or even upside down. The significance of each may be left to your imagination!

* * *

The amazing rise in the popularity of Teddy Bears has caused them to leap up the list of most collected objects—they are now fourth, behind coins, stamps and dolls. And on the rare occasions when vintage bears come up for sale at the auctions held by houses like Sotheby's and Christie's in New York and London, the prices can be quite staggering. It's yet another factor in the amazing development of 'bear awareness'.

Just how amazing is revealed by Susie Mayor, the charming head of the Dolls and Tedtiles (sorry, Textiles) Department at Christie's in South Kensington, London.

'In the past two or three years, interest has grown tremendously in collecting soft toys, teddies especially,' she says. 'It still seems to be increasing and prices are rising. One of the problems is that, on the whole, most teddies have been rather loved, so they may be damaged. If they have lost some fur from being hugged it is not so

The hug of bears auctioned at Sotheby's in October 1984.

important. It does detract from their worth, though, if they have been badly repaired. In fact, it is very rare—and rather sad—to find one in mint condition.'

Over at Phillips' Auction Rooms, their Teddy Bear expert Anna Marret is able to confirm that they, too, have become aware of the soaring demand for vintage teddies. Indeed, in August 1984, an 80-year-old bear manufactured by the pioneering German firm of Steiff, with the maker's unmistakable button label in his left ear and a quite menacing growl still fully operational, was snapped up with a bid of £420! Yes, Anna agrees, old teddies are coming out of the woods (or perhaps attics) to attract very eager bidding.

'It's the early bears that collectors want, of course,' she says. 'The ones which are immediately recognisable by the humps on the back where the stuffing was finished. But the hump vanished as techniques improved, so now a teddy with a hump and the original growl mechanism is very much in demand. Another important factor is the bear's character—that can be absolutely decisive.

'The problem is that it is often difficult to obtain an accurate guide of the age of a Teddy Bear. Bears up to the mid-1930s will feel hard, being filled with straw, although they are covered in brown plush, a cloth which looks like fur. They are more likely to have glass eyes, a pointed nose, and often a voice on a balance mechanism. Plus, of course, jointed arms, legs and head.'

It would be pointless to try and give any guidelines here as to the value of old Teddy Bears, as the prices are constantly changing and any list would certainly be out of date before this book appeared. But just as an indication, here are some prices reached at a couple of recent auctions.

At Sotheby's third teddy sale in October 1984, the top bear dated from around 1920. He was 41 inches high with a pink-brown plush body, and as something of a novelty he had a growler

The blonde Steiff bear made about 1905 which sold for the world-record figure of £2,090 at Sotheby's in May 1985.

in each arm. He was sold for £286, double the estimate. A 24-inch English teddy manufactured around 1910 made £176 (estimate £150–£200), and Chad, the teddy made around 1955 to advertise Bear Brand stockings, brought £275 (estimate £100–£150). Only a stuffed English giant panda of around 1950 fell below its estimate of £60–£80, going for just £38.50.

It was a similar story of booming prices at Phillips' in February 1985, where the highlight was a Steiff pale plush bear with button eyes, a black hump and swivel eyes which set a new auction record of £1,210 against an estimate of just £100–£150! It was an American dealer who made the record offer—even though the bear's pads had been renewed and he had lost a bit of stuffing—and the man had to bid against fierce competition from a London-based private collector.

Another Steiff teddy, with a growler that no longer worked and worn pads, still made £660 against estimates of £100–£200. The American dealer also paid £374 for a similar straw-stuffed plush teddy which Phillips' were unable to attribute to any specific manufacturer. Again the price was over three times the estimates! The entire sale made a massive total of £45,536.*

With such interest being evinced, it is not surprising to learn that the auction houses are planning to be very selective in the future about the bears they offer for sale. Sotheby's, for instance, will only take pre-1930 teddies, and the others are equally concerned about age and quality.

This said, we believe it is unlikely that there will be a flood of teddies on the market, because parting with an old friend is a terrible wrench in any circumstances. How can even a substantial sum of money make up for all those years of comfort? Even though there is a new breed of dealers doing their best to part people from their teddies, we think a bigger area of growth will be

* As we were going to press, a new record for a Teddy Bear was set at Sotheby's on May 21, 1985. A Steiff blonde teddy of around 1905 was sold for £2,090 (estimate £300–£500). It had a black-stitched pointed snout, black button eyes, a hump, swivel joints and was clothed in a white dress.

in the fields of bear memorabilia such as postcards, books, china ware, song sheets and such like.

Beware, though, for Teddy Bear hunters are on the prowl. Not long after our previous book was published, advertisements began to appear in such newspapers as *The Times* and the *Daily Telegraph.* One in the *Daily Telegraph*, placed by an American dealer who called himself Mr Smith of San Francisco, appealed enticingly, 'Teddy Bears Wanted. Old jointed Teddy Bears and related teddy items. Send price, description, and photo. Agents also wanted to find Teddy Bears.'

Not surprisingly, we protested about such activities to the newspapers, and the Londoner's Diary column in *The New Standard* made our protest the lead item. Generously calling our book, 'the definitive work on the subject,' the newspaper thundered:

'Horrid news for arctophiles! Pots of money are being offered to induce them to part with their Teddy Bears. So bad is the situation becoming, that one seasoned owner told me this morning that Britain seems to be gripped by a bear hug.'

But already, said the columnist, he detected signs of a fight back against the insidious advertisers, and after hearing our feelings, contacted a couple of other teddy lovers, Peter Bull, and a most influential member of the House of Lords, Lord Lyell.

'It is bear-faced robbery,' hurrumphed Peter in his best outraged voice. 'Once Teddy Bears are made homeless they are prey for this sort of unscrupulous dealer. They just have nowhere to go.'

Lord Lyell, the Government Spokesman on Employment and Scottish Affairs, was equally forthright.

'This is outrageous behaviour,' he said, 'Why, my own chums, Jimmy and Thumper, travel everywhere with me. I've had them for over 40 years and I couldn't bear to think of them falling into the wrong hands. "Hands Off Our Teddy Bears!" is what I say.'

Another of our good friends in the House, Lord Bath, even came up with a positive suggestion for teddies under threat. He would open up a Teddy Bear squat at Longleat!

In fact the publicity worked well, and it was not long after that an English dealer searching for vintage teddies told the *Daily Mirror* how little success he was having:

'There's a great market in the States for renovated traditional Teddy Bears,' said Paul Burns of Aldershot, 'and we're prepared to pay up to £10 each (!) for old ones. But we've had little response because people get so attached to their bears.'

Burns added that despite widespread advertising and personal contact, his bear hunt had produced just one bear. The story made us smile—it was just one more example of Bear Power.

* * *

What has been called the 'swankiest bear event of the year' is the annual 'Take a Teddy to Tea Society' which meets at the famous old New York hotel, the Algonquin, on the anniversary of A.A. Milne's birthday.

On one occasion, the original bear belonging to Milne's son, Christopher Robin, popped into this gathering, as did the splendidly named Savoyard-Winnistrand-Pooh, the resident bear of London's Savoy Hotel who flew over by Concorde to attend. Peter Bull's friend, Aloysius, was also an honoured guest, having come fresh from Hollywood where he had put his paws into the cement outside Grauman's Chinese Theatre to earn a little slice of immortality alongside all those other famous show business names—the only Teddy Bear to have done so!

Another remarkable furry chap who usually puts in appearances at these gatherings is Moretonhampstead, who belongs to the New York cartoonist, Gahan Wilson, and his wife Nancy Winters. One cannot help feeling a little ashamed of one's fellow Britons on hearing Nancy describe how they found the little teddy neglected and looking very sorry for himself on one of their visits to England. They decided he deserved better things and paid the princely sum of just five pence to rescue him for a better life. And what a better life!

'He goes everywhere with us,' Nancy says. 'He's been on the

A small part of the huge crowd of Teddy Bear lovers who have made the Longleat gatherings such a success.

QE2 and the Orient Express. He also corresponds regularly with Pierre Cardin who calls him "Ted-ee". He's a very *soigné* bear—the more jaded you are, the more amused you are by Moretonhampstead!'

* * *

Commercialism is becoming increasingly evident in the world of the Teddy Bear. Apart from the ever growing ranges of new teddies (including Steiff's latest model called 'Petsy' which they claim is fully machine washable), the Americans have created an organisation called Pillow Talk Inc which will call on you before you go to sleep, tuck you up with a teddy loaned for the night, and even read a bedtime story if required! The Japanese have introduced 'Pot Bellies', a line of teddies with very fat stomachs which make them 'extra-cuddly', it is claimed, while a British electronics expert, Andrew Page, has produced 'Snoozy Bear', a teddy with a tiny electronic oscillator circuit and loudspeaker which reproduces the sound heard by an unborn child in the womb and is said to settle even the most fractious baby. This 'Bionic Ted' has certainly impressed midwives and paediatricians, and in a test carried out in a London maternity unit, 23 crying infants were soothed to sleep or else wide-eyed contentment when 'Snoozy' was placed in their cots.

An Illinois inventor, Louis Stangle, has taken this idea a step further and designed speaking bears that tell business executives how wonderful they are! There are separate teddies for men or women, but both encourage their owners to 'be what you want to be. You're on your way to the top—you're a born leader. You're perfect, just perfect!'

Talking to the press after the rapid sale of 300,000 of the 'Executive Bears', Mr Stangle said, 'The mission of the bears is to make people happy and tell them things they want to hear at the end of a busy day. I believe that's what they do—as well as offering the feeling of comfort that is inherent in all Teddy Bears.'

* * *

Of course, no world is ever perfect, and it is almost unbearable to have to report that there have been occasions when teddies have got hurt. There was a horrible story in the autumn of 1983, when fans of the San Diego Padres hanged thousands of small bears in effigy after their baseball team had been badly beaten in the

The biggest teddy of them all? The Sunday Mirror's *Big Ted with a young admirer, also at Longleat.*

NGLEAT
SUNDAY MAY 27th
EAT TEDDY BEAR RALLY
and HONEY
FAIR
LONGLEA
SUNDAY MAY 27th
THE GREAT TEDDY BEAR
and HONEY
FAIR

National League playoffs (as if it had been *their* fault!), while three ladies who really should have known better actually hit a five-foot teddy with baseball clubs in front of the bus carrying the Chicago Cubs team, to vent their anger at the men's performance. It's also true that teddies have been used to smuggle all manner of things through the customs, and there can be no particular pleasure in recording that one large bear was recently unceremoniously slit open at Rio Airport, to reveal 500 pairs of silk knickers!

There was also the little matter of a British drain-clearing firm who claimed recently that teddies were the biggest cause of blocked drains and therefore must be 'the most hated of children's toys'.

'In a survey we conducted we discovered that the Teddy Bear was always the one toy that ended up in the toilet,' said a spokesman. 'Of course, there were others, but the teddy is way ahead of the rest. And it is a very difficult thing to do. An awful lot of feeling must have gone into it!'

It must be said in reply, and with equal feeling, that the Teddy Bear is certainly *not* the most hated of creatures; such occurrences can be explained by the fits of temper to which all children are suddenly victim and which they just as quickly regret.

On the lighter side, one must mention the teddy, appropriately named 'Porridge', made by the inmates of Dartmoor Prison. He was created in August 1979 and proved the first in a long line of bears made by the prisoners for sale to raise money for children's charities.

The idea of the prisoners making bears was started by the assistant governor, David Pike. He quickly found that even men from among the 30 serving life sentences could not resist the challenge.

'They are all getting a real kick out of this,' David said. 'They are all interested to know where their bears go and how much they raise. Already we've made several thousand pounds for children's charities and are planning to produce even more ambitious Teddy Bears in the future.'

If ever there was an example of Teddy Bear Power this is it!

One could go on almost indefinitely with stories like these about the extraordinary appeal and influence of the Teddy Bear. Our little friend has proved his worth and, like a fine Persian carpet, improves with age. He is the childhood friend who sticks to you through life, and is actually all the better for being bare of fur, minus an eye and with a well-worn patch or two. He makes the transition from nursery to boudoir with effortless ease, and possesses a character that lifts him just as easily into the realm of being a person.

We hope we've shown you in these pages a little of *what* makes the Teddy Bear so appealing, and a lot about *why* he does. Teddy Bear affection is certainly all around, and by being 'bear aware' you can share in it yourself. If you still have any doubts, then watch out.

Because anyone can be taken unawares . . . by Teddy Bears!

August, 1985

THE GOOD BEARS' GUIDE

Here are some useful addresses for Teddy Bears and their friends.

CLUBS
Good Bears of the World
Headquarters: PO Box 8236, Honolulu, Hawaii 96815.
United Kingdom Den, 17, Barnton Gardens, Edinburgh EH4 6AF.
Paddington's Make It Grow Club
c/o Action Research, Vincent House, Horsham, West Sussex.
International Teddy Bear Club
1 Dyers Buildings, Holborn, London EC1N 2JT.

MUSEUMS
The National Toy Museum, The Royal Pavilion, Art Gallery and Museum, Brighton.
The Museum of Childhood, Cambridge Heath Road, Bethnal Green, London, E2.
Pollock's Toy Museum, 1 Scala Street, London, W1.
The Museum of Childhood, High Street, Edinburgh.

HOSPITALS
The Bristol Dolls' Hospital, Alpha Road, Southville, Bristol.
The London Dolls' Hospital, 16 Dawes Road, London, SW6.
The American Dolls' Hospital, 787 Lexington Avenue, New York.